COMMANDING
heights

COMMUNITY
control

NEW ECONOMICS
FOR A NEW
SOUTH AFRICA

PATRICK
BOND

Ravan Press   Johannesburg

Published by Ravan Press (Pty) Ltd
PO Box 31134
Braamfontein
2017
South Africa

© Patrick Bond

First published April 1991

Cover illustration by Erica Hibbert

ISBN 0 86975 407 6

Printed by Clyson Printers, 11th Avenue, Maitland

Contents

CONTENTS

Preface

Extraordinary economic power has been centralised and exercised at the 'commanding heights' of South Africa's economy. As a consequence of that power, many unjust acts have been committed by state planning departments, mining houses and financial institutions – not only against the country's masses of poor and working people, but also against those attempting to forge a productive path for specifically *capitalist* development.

South Africa's 40 million people currently live in a warped economic environment, characterised both by grotesque inequality and depravation for which the country is world renowned, and by a host of lesser-known maladies: long-term manufacturing recession; agricultural overproduction and debt crisis; extreme rationalisation throughout industry; an explosion of financial speculation and consumer credit which is far beyond what is usual in a normal economy; and a generally unpatriotic big business class which has pulled billions of rands out of the economy in recent years. These are some of the worst problems which have afflicted South Africa's private sector. And this does not take note of the irrationalities, racism and outright corruption that permeate the public sector.

Because the 'Great Economic Debate' hinges so much on the relative merits of public sector versus business sector production, it is useful to understand, historically, the close linkage between the two in the development of apartheid capitalism. This is the object of Chapter One, while Chapter Two makes clear that both the current state and big business are responding to the contemporary economic crisis with broadly compatible strategies. I stress the importance of an accurate analysis of economic crisis, and use the concept of 'over-accumulation' to provide a different interpretation to that found in most mainstream and radical theories.

Differences between the mainstream crisis-management strategy and the evolving Growth through Redistribution programme of the ANC and Cosatu are the subject of Chapter Three. Both these 'solutions' to the economic crisis, I argue, may fall short of addressing the economy's deep-rooted problems. In Chapter Four, I consider some antidotes to economic power directed from the commanding heights, under the rubric of 'community control'. This involves struggles in workplaces, townships and even international financial districts. The philosophy of community control entails less than revolutionary socialism, but certainly more than the likely compromise outcome between big business and the nationalist movement. Community control of capital suggests real, ongoing forms of resistance to the excesses of those at the commanding heights.

Commanding heights and community control are two powerful windows on economic development, and involve complementary arenas of political struggle. They come together in conflict during moments of economic crisis – moments which have increasingly overwhelmed the development of South African capitalism since the late 1960s (and also at other times in the country's history).

It is here that forces far beyond the control of ordinary South Africans shape living and working conditions, the policies of government, and even society's ideological climate. Communities, however defined, have often tried to resist these forces, but have never been wholly successful. This is largely because, directed from the commanding heights, flows of capital through key sectors of the economy and society have been decisive. Community control of capital is, fundamentally, about addressing the most damaging flows of capital and in the process gaining as much power over the broader economy as is realistically possible.

These, then, are the twin themes of this study, contributing to at least one round (the ideological) in the struggle for the South African economy. Some of the arguments advanced are original, extending beyond standard radical interpretations of economic crisis. And although some strategies and tactics of campaigns for community control have been explored in progressive publications, there has been little effort to tie these struggles into an understanding of the economic crisis. This book can only be considered a first step in this regard, but will hopefully lead to further considerations along these lines.

It is extremely taxing to write eloquently about the economy, especially when focusing on obscure financial processes organised behind closed doors which are rarely felt directly by ordinary people. This makes it tempting to glamourise the world of money by highlighting the unique, spectacular characteristics of some of the major agents of economic power, whether individuals or institutions. There is no shortage of such case material in South Africa.

This practice, though, often leads to the idea that history is created by great men, women or companies. It tends to downplay much larger social forces, especially the economic imperatives to which even the most powerful individual actors are mere servants.

If one is attempting to unveil the pernicious activities of South Africa's capitalist elites in a way that is politically and theoretically accessible and meaningful, then a knife-edge course must somehow be cut between agency and structure.

To this end, I have drawn arguments from numerous well-researched though somewhat obscure radical academic studies, and am appreciative of the rich legacy of historical and contemporary work on South Africa's political economy.

Apologies must be made on two counts. First, social science research has drawn our attention to all manner of particularities which contradict easy theoretically-derived cliches, and to factors that are irreducible to the laws of motion of capital, and these have not been adequately incorporated in a text suffering from severe space limitations. Second, this also explains the lack of formal citations, footnotes, and other paraphernalia of the academy.

Instead, the style is one of journalism, in which the verification for novel arguments must rely upon a few descriptive statistics and quotes from interviews, public statements, speeches and the media. These quotes are meant, in the tradition of balanced reporting, to provide the reader with a number of points of view on a particular issue. This means that wherever possible, representatives of business or of mainstream economics (eg Schumann, Henry, Osborn) are given opportunity to comment, even where a vastly different conclusion is reached.

Acknowledgements

Naturally, a few comradely disagreements remain with those who have helped me dissect the South African economy these last few months, but I am unreservedly grateful to the many progressive thinkers who have spent time helping guide this project. There was special encouragement and help from Dana, Charles, Malcolm, Jenny, Nicoli, Alan, Darlene, Greg, Avril, Moss, Suzi, Tim, Miriam, Mark, Billy, Meshack, Stephen, Jonny, Kate, Paul and the members of the 'Johannesburg Regulation Theory and Urbanisation Reading Group.' Beneficial feedback was also drawn from presentations to the African Studies Institute of the University of the Witwatersrand, Khanya College, Cosatu's Economic Trends group, and PLANACT. Resonance from a number of grassroots trade unionists and community leaders was invaluable, especially in shaping the way the arguments developed. Ingrid and Glenn were kind and patient editors, while Stan, Blake and Denis were excellent guides to township society and politics. And my appreciation for the intellectual work of David Harvey and Simon Clarke cannot be overstated.

I would like to acknowledge a series of interviews and discussions with executives, including economists, of the Johannesburg Stock Exchange and some JSE brokerage firms, Anglo American Corporation, several major financial institutions, the Urban Foundation, the Chamber of Mines, the Democratic and Conservative Parties, various departments of the South African government and Inkatha. For their time I am grateful. But I can only hope to have made some contribution towards the undoing of their sundry rationalisations and defences of the privileges that have accumulated so unjustly at the South African economy's commanding heights.

Patrick Bond
Johannesburg, November 1990

Introduction

The scene is a downtown Johannesburg boardroom in the plush headquarters of one of South Africa's huge conglomerates. Several well-dressed men sit around the shining mahogany table, glumly looking at their company's latest income statements.

'Bad news, gentlemen. Following a brief upturn in the late 1980s, profits are down again, with no improvement in sight,' says the grim-faced managing director, now beginning to display the tension he feels inside. He looks at each of the men in turn.

'We're going to need to take some drastic steps. Bob, can we pull out of that benefits deal with the union in Durban? What about the plan to get 10% more output from the production line? And is our subcontracting strategy in place yet? What about that new Japanese inventory system everyone's talking about? We have to cut costs out there, man!

'And Mike, can we close down that East Rand factory and move it to the Ciskei? We'd get several hundred thou in government subsidies, and the workers there will be a pushover.

'Who's supposed to be looking at international acquisitions? Didn't I make it clear enough, Johann? We've got to develop more options in Europe, as soon as possible. I'm talking hundreds of millions that the directors allocated to getting us off this miserable continent.

'Hey Andre, on these debt repayment problems we're having – are you looking for some more short-term credit to keep the banks happy? I don't care how much it costs, damn it, borrow if you have to from overseas on our line of trade credit. Can you sell some of our speculative securities? Or how about dumping that Cape Town real estate we thought would skyrocket in price last year?

'Jim, the big insurance company shareholders are screaming bloody murder about the last dividend payout. We've got to stop the haemorrhaging in our manufacturing division. Henk, what about arranging a merger of that division with Anglo's shop? The Competition Board will probably let us get away with it.

'The bottom line is this. We've just got to come up with some quick cash from somewhere, because that ANC team is knocking at our door. Jabu in PRO says he thinks we'll have to contribute at least 50 million to this big Consultative Business Movement social responsibility fund.'

This is not unusual talk. Like many poor and working people, corporate leaders are sweating as the 1990s get underway. Their economy is in bad shape, with customers cutting back on orders and falling behind on payments, major banks on the edge of failure, and other big problems ahead. The corporate chiefs must expand their markets, switch technology to become internationally competitive, and still keep the cheap foreign imports at bay. The unions are a constant thorn in their sides, and the prospect of an African National Congress government is not a happy one.

But firms at the commanding heights of the economy have much more power to resolve their problems than ordinary people do. They control the flows of funds in the economy; the bulk of manufacturing output; the raw materials in the ground and on the land; the direction of trade and commerce; contacts with the international economy; the way in which cities develop; and the sorts of labour-management practices that become the norm across industry.

The South African Reserve Bank – responsible for all the money circulating in the economy – is at the financial peak of the commanding heights. A group of commercial banks (Standard, First National, Bankorp, Nedbank, Volkskas, etc) and insurance companies (Old Mutual, Sanlam, Liberty Life, Southern Life, etc) controlling several hundred billion rands in credit and long-term investments, stand alongside it. And these are closely related to – and in many cases, owned by – the half-dozen major mining-related conglomerates.

None is more important than the Anglo American and De Beers empire, which includes a host of other mines, as well as firms specialising in industry, commerce, property, finance, and even agriculture. The Sanlam group comes next, with a major bank (Bankorp), mining company (Gencor), building society (Saambou) and an entire range of other commercial ventures under its wing. Interconnections between these giants and other conglomerates abound: Barlow Rand, Volkskas, Rembrandt, Anglovaal and Iscor. Still other firms are owned by the state (Eskom, Transnet, Posts and Telecommunications, Foscor, the Land Bank, etc), though before long, they may be sold – 'privatised' – to big investors.

Fairly anonymous, uncontroversial state bureaucrats have the helm of many state agencies. But even men with dull personalities can play a crucial role in the economy because the institutions they lead are so powerful. More interesting are the moguls of private companies, since their own egos and personalities were important in their firms' climb to the top.

All of them, however – firms and people – are subject to the rules of capitalist markets and competition. It is these that the managing director of our Johannesburg conglomerate is cursing.

The scene shifts half-way across the country to a much less fancy room, in a remote corner of the Transkei, where dismissed and retrenched members of the National Union of Mineworkers are talking to union organisers about their economic situation.

'There were no jobs in our village. The land was very bad. We have families. So we came to the mines.' Mbulelo Dubu, a worker leader, has thought a lot about his economic problems.

He works for Vaal Reefs, which is owned by the Anglo American Corporation, South Africa's biggest company. He uses some of his pay packet to buy things he needs, and sends the rest to his family in Natal. After working in the mines all week, Dubu wants to relax. He buys a newspaper made with paper from Mondi, an Anglo company. While catching up on the news, he drinks a beer – whether a Castle, Lion or Hansa – and the profits go to South African Breweries, partly owned by Anglo. When he buys clothes from Edgars, his money again trickles back to SA Breweries, and then to Anglo.

His wife, Mary, spends the money she receives from Mbulelo at her local shop in a remote village. She buys sugar made by Tongaat-Hulett, also part of the Anglo stable. Mielie meal she buys comes from Premier Milling, again largely Anglo-owned. The local shopkeeper makes a profit from sales to people like Mary, which he puts toward a Samcor truck, sold by McCarthy's. Again, Anglo gets the profits.

What about Dubu's pension, which he will get when he retires? For the moment, it is used by First National Bank (owned by Anglo). Mbulelo Dubu has no control over FNB, and no choice over what his capital is used for. He is not even aware that his money is invested by the bank in the Johannesburg Stock Exchange (JSE), where stocks seem to be rising in price.

But the manufacturing companies that appear so strong on the JSE are beginning to wilt. Since they have not been ploughing profits back into machinery and new factories, it is possible that their JSE value will collapse, leaving Dubu and other pensioners out in the cold.

The NUM organiser sums up this sorry situation: 'Only a small amount of your pay check will help your family and village develop. You need to spend most of your pay just to stay alive, and the profits go to the big producers without helping ordinary people around you. The office buildings in the cities grow bigger as a result, but the poor areas stay just the same. In the office buildings, bankers take the money and put it into investments that do no one any good.'

Dubu realises he has virtually no control over the capital that is flowing all around him. Can he change this situation?

The NUM organiser offers one possible alternative. She talks about village co-operatives and the potential they have for development. In a small rural village, Meshack, a migrant worker on the mines, wants to get married. Instead of going to Ellerines to buy furniture, he goes to the carpentry co-op and buys a good bed. The co-op members decide to buy chickens from the village poultry co-op with their profits. The workers in the poultry co-op are becoming more and more prosperous, and can now afford to send their children to school. A sewing co-op in the village makes their uniforms.

'The money does not simply go in one end and out the other,' says the organiser. 'It circulates around in the village, and more jobs are created.' This village co-operative network is one of NUM's responses to the economic crisis affecting the mining industry. At least 100 000 miners are in the process of losing their jobs because international mineral prices remain low, more mines have been exhausted, and new machinery is replacing workers.

The co-operative network is a clear illustration of community control of capital. It is an extremely small example of resistance against the economy's commanding heights, but it gives Mbulelo Dubu and other mineworkers an idea about the hidden forces that affect their lives, and demonstrates that miners do have a capacity to intervene in their own interests.

The example of Meshack's village is, of course, an idealised model, not yet in existence. There are numerous barriers to the vision of capital circulating in rural villages, and the development of linkages between co-operatives will be a long, gruelling process. But the vision is there, and some very energetic people are working hard to make it a reality.

NUM is also engaged in complex negotiations with mining companies. The union attack has included everything from international sanctions pressure to sophisticated corporate campaigns. Although none of these economic strategies are as far-reaching as the union's demand for nationalisation of the mines, such attempts to gain some power in the South African economy have great potential.

In the months following President FW de Klerk's dramatic 2 February 1990 speech, the question of the post-apartheid economy became very important. Economists and others who earlier would have nothing to do with each other participated in 'The Great Economic Debate'. A half-dozen books on the economy were quickly published, nearly all of them advocating a free market (or at most social democratic) solution to questions about the economic future. Progressives began isolating the fundamental principles, and some mechanisms, to enshrine social justice and racial equality.

But in the haste to think about what to do with the post-apartheid economy, a few important points began to be lost:

◆ What is South Africa's economic inheritance? How did the economy develop over the past couple of centuries? Who gained and who lost?

◆ How did the current problems in the economy evolve? Where did the rot begin, and what have those at the commanding heights been doing to halt it these past couple of decades?

◆ What do those at the commanding heights have in mind for the near future? What are they telling the ANC to do? Are they getting their way? Where are they vulnerable? And are there any flaws in the economic programme of the ANC and Cosatu? Is it feasible for these progressive organisations to nurse an economy in crisis back to health? Or will they merely inherit the burden of cracking down on poor and working people?

◆ How does the debate over the economy relate to struggles at the grassroots – from townships to the shopfloor to the international anti-apartheid movement? Is there a logic to these struggles? Can the grassroots campaigns play a role in the resolution of South Africa's national economic crisis, and affect the direction of the world economy?

These are the questions posed in the following pages. South Africa has an opportunity unusual in world history. The liberation struggle has involved millions of people, and the expectations for substantial changes are high. Workers are well organised in many sectors of the economy, and township residents are flexing their muscles in ways that the state and some private companies have been unable to resist. If South Africa's vast majority of poor and working people use the principles of community control to build a strong local economy, if the South African foreign debt is used wisely, and if gold plays its traditional role during economic crisis, then there is every chance for a progressive post-apartheid government to have an important impact far beyond its own borders.

To find out why this is the case, we must examine the economic inheritance the first democratic South African government will have to overcome. Companies at the commanding heights have been building their power for well over a century, and to dislodge that power we must first understand its origins.

1

The inheritance

South Africa's current economic crisis is not only a result of the recent past. Looting and plunder, expropriation of land and property, formal and informal racism, sexism, and super-exploitation of labour have played fundamental roles in making the South African economy what it is today. A backward glance at history is therefore necessary both to understand the economic crisis, and propose solutions for a democratic way out of it.

Certain features of the economic inheritance come to the fore again and again: rampant speculation and financial gambling, unnecessary ties to imperialism, unreasonable levels of monopolisation, and – especially in recent days – huge withdrawals of local capital which have done more long-term damage to the future South African economy than even international economic sanctions.

History shows that the current problems of growth have, in one form or another, been experienced before.

These problems arise, not because of an overly-interfering government, nor even because of popular resistance by poor and working people. Rather, the economy is going through an investment crisis and economic slump because of purely capitalist processes that can be traced to the very commanding heights of the economy.

To quote Nedbank's chief economist, Edward Osborn, 'We've brought about our own cause of poor growth. We've imposed our own sanctions on ourselves through this unwillingness to invest.'

Probing this legacy will be resisted by some, certainly, like Anglo American's Gavin Relly. 'Let us not dwell on the past,' he pleaded to a meeting of ANC and business representatives who met in mid-1990 to discuss ways of resolving the economic crisis.

'Relly can afford not to dwell on the past,' the ANC responded, 'because that past has made him rich and powerful. This is not the case for the majority of South Africans, who have suffered and still suffer as a result of that past.'

Merchant capital

Merchants, not miners or farmers, initially introduced capitalism to South Africa and linked it to the world economy. Prior to the 1870s, international traders unmistakably shaped the economy of the Cape and the interior, and when British merchant banks arrived in the 1860s, imperialism was rapidly imposed

High finance

*F*rom the early 19th century, high finance – first as an excessive surge of government-issued cash and then the spread of banks – had enormous impact on the South African economy.

Early in British colonial rule, the policy of 'loose money' – government willingness to print currency without calculating the effects on the economy – devalued local currency dramatically. Consequent price increases ('inflation') damaged local and international trade. Control of the Cape's economy soon shifed from the colonial government to private banks, which proved even more harmful.

Economic historian CGW Schumann remarked, in his pathbreaking study of South African business cycles, that early booms and collapses in the Cape were 'evidently of a *purely financial and speculative character.* It reminds us strongly of the speculative manias during the 18th century in Europe and England, especially the South Sea Bubble of 1720. They might with some justification be called the growing diseases of a rising Capitalism.'

But the speculative disease was more than just a problem of youthful, rising capitalism. It reflected deep-rooted tendencies that exist in even the most mature capitalist economies.

upon the South African economy. Settlers – first Dutch, then British – had arrived in increasing numbers since 1652, partly because of unhappy conditions associated with industrialisation and unemployment in Europe.

Many Cape Africans who did not flee north or east ended up as slaves. The Cape's position on a premier world trade route was increasingly important, and a landowning class arose which supplied agricultural products to international traders. By the 19th century this class dominated other whites, who subsisted largely on stock farming.

African tribes consolidated in the face of settler expansion, and by the time of the great trek north in 1836, five main African kingdoms had formed. For many years they presented staunch resistance to colonial expansion, and shaped the path of settlement. But the settlers' superior arms were generally the deciding factor.

The expropriation of African land and livestock escalated, especially after the 1850-53 frontier war. The Xhosa people were also weakened, and propelled into the settler economy by a traumatic cattle-killing movement. Development of the region was uneven, but proceeded rapidly.

Racism and economic oppression of indigenous people prevailed. In spite of the settlers' extensive ideological and religious efforts to veil racism as God-given or natural, it had a striking material basis in settler survival strategies and their uneasy relationship with imperialism.

The root of the problem lay less with people as individuals, and more in the economic system that drove them forward to new geographic conquests. For example, from the early 1800s, the settler economy was profoundly influenced by a local form of 'high finance.'

Standard pricks the economic bubble

Standard Bank quickly became the entire region's dominant financial institution. Shortly before the 1881 financial panic, one Standard inspector in Kimberley glibly pronounced, 'There does not appear to have been much in the shape of rash speculation in this place, and I believe business to be healthy.'

Matters were made worse when the bank realised its mistakes, as Standard's official biographer, JA Henry, admits. Notwithstanding his commitment to the diamond trade, the bank's first general manager was chiefly to blame for the severity of the 1881 crash. 'Robert Stewart decided that the time had come to call a halt' to what was indeed rash speculation, reports Henry.

'It cannot have escaped him that in doing so he would expose his bank, and South African banks in general, to an intense degree of embittered opprobrium, corresponding to the inflated hopes of the bubble which he was about to prick. Fortunately he was a brave man.

'What Robert Stewart could not have foreseen without an inhuman degree of second sight,' Henry goes on, 'was that his pricking of the bubble would coincide with the onset of an almost unexampled depression in other fields of the South African economy.'

This interference was not taken lightly, especially by farmers driven to ruin. The Afrikaner Bond gained some political mileage from bank-bashing, claiming in the early 1880s that bankers were 'draining the country,' and even going so far as starting their own banks in Stellenbosch and Hopetown. Standard responded to the populist anger by officially dropping 'British' from its name in 1883.

Minerals and wage labour

With the discovery of diamonds in 1867 and the rapid growth of mining companies, the economy changed rapidly. Britain became extremely interested in the colony, and supported full colonisation of the African kingdoms, which was largely completed by 1881.

Nothing was more important in South Africa's economic and social history than the mineral wealth discovered first in Kimberley and then in the enormous gold deposits of the Witwatersrand in 1886. This windfall governed the development of labour relations, the formation of classes, and the nature of local corporate power.

Migrant labour was introduced in a form that would last a century. 'Colour bars' and job classifications were set up, African workers completely enclosed in compounds for the duration of contracts, pass laws instituted, and recruitment systems developed. Wage labour and other characteristics of capitalist relations were established in mining, and then became entrenched in agriculture and manufacturing.

Prior to the opening of the diamond finds, people of all races had made their living primarily off the land. Mining developed at a time of world-wide depression, and quickly became a magnet for white immigration. So while Africans were by and large coerced into wage labour, for whites the process was more voluntary.

To support the mineral industry, many other economic sectors burgeoned: transport, communications, agriculture, stock farming, trade and finance. Britain quickly enlarged the political boundaries of the Cape to encompass the diamond mines and by 1876 a telegraph connected Kimberley with Cape Town. Following the Transvaal gold discoveries, railroad construction joined the Witwatersrand to the Cape in 1892 and to Mozambique in 1895.

These advances – especially networking between towns – were mainly the doings of bankers in Cape Town and Port Elizabeth, whose vision and control of funds surpassed those of even the colonial government.

Miners and financiers

In the search for the richest deposits of gold, mineworkers were forced ever deeper into the earth during the 1890s. Labour was always in short supply, although military conquest throughout the region brought South Africa huge new supplies of migrant workers. By the time deep-level mining was introduced, around 60% of African mineworkers were Mozambican.

More and more sophisticated equipment was needed to extract the gold. Companies realised that they would have to grow much faster to pay for expensive shaft-sinking equipment, milling and extraction plant, and labour, which covered 60% of total costs.

'Monopoly capitalism' developed, involving close collusion between some 30 major gold producers, and their organisation into groups responsible for technical,

Financial power and diamond speculation

*B*y the 1880s – a time of South Africa's two most devastating financial panics – economic power was concentrated in a few financial institutions which controlled credit and capital. These were the Cape banks (especially Standard) and, increasingly in the 1880s, the mining houses born in the Kimberley diamond fields.

As the 1873-95 world economic crisis began, foreign investor confidence in South Africa – led by the Rothschilds – was high. It was unaffected even by minor wars waged by the British against Africans and Afrikaners, which stimulated the South African economy because the British pumped in millions of pounds to ensure victory.

One round of serious fighting resulted from the Cape colony's 1877 invasion and annexation of the Transvaal republic. That brief annexation has been traced in part to the powerful Cape Commercial Bank's problems in getting Transvaal government loans repaid. Once annexation occurred the Standard Bank immediately moved to set up branches in Potchefstroom and Pretoria. Financial power and local politics were closely related.

But, says CGW Schumann, that did not prevent disastrous mismanagement of the economy: 'Unsound banking practices, over and above the natural credit expansion inherent in an elastic monetary system, had greatly contributed to the over-intensity of the boom, while the rapid curtailment of credit after 1881 must be considered as the main cause of the extreme severity of the depression.

'There can be little doubt that the banks had acted indiscreetly. They were severely criticised at the time, and the criticism was largely justified. The undesirability of having bank directors overseas, who did not know local conditions well enough and who were apt to apply the banking principles of an established industrialised country, especially during the period of depression, to a young developing country, became very clear during this time.'

administrative and financial rationalisation. The next stage was a wave of mergers which resulted in six huge companies – Consolidated Gold Fields, Rand Mines, General Mining, Central Mining, Union Corporation, and Johannesburg Consolidated Investments.

Each had mining, exploration and prospecting arms, and boards of directors in Johannesburg and London. From these beginnings, the mining houses achieved an extraordinary expertise in shifting ownership shares and key executive personnel among various related companies to ensure maximum control over the development of the economy.

But in the mining industry's first few decades, labour was the key issue. The Chamber of Mines was founded to help co-ordinate the mining capitalists, and its special responsibility was forcing African wages down. It lobbied the government for help in recruiting labour and for a tough pass system to prevent Africans from deserting the mines.

'Private enterprise has repeatedly failed in attempting to organise and maintain an adequate supply of Kaffirs,' the Chamber pleaded to President Kruger in 1890. 'The task must be undertaken by the public authorities, and the Chamber trusts that the Government will lend it their indispensable assistance.'

White workers were not treated as poorly by the mining companies. As recent immigrants from Europe many had a strong trade union consciousness, and were involved more with construction and development than actual digging, thus giving them a better bargaining position. To overcome labour problems and invest in deep-level mining, the mining giants required ever greater amounts of money. Much of the fresh cash was raised in London, and to a lesser extent on the Paris, Vienna and Berlin stock exchanges. Over the course of the next half century, the mines offered extremely attractive profits to foreign financiers.

By 1895 speculation again reached fever-pitch in South Africa, according to the Standard Bank's JA Henry. 'The market value of South African shares quoted on the London Stock Exchange, which had stood at less than £20-million at the beginning of 1894, had risen to over £55-million by the end of that year. The movement continued without interruption for nine months more, so that the figure of £55-million was itself trebled.

'Nor was speculation entirely confined to shares,' says Henry. 'Land and property in Johannesburg were also changing hands at fantastic prices and the whole town was in a fever of excitement.'

But with English-Afrikaner tensions heavy in the air and the Jameson Raid imminent, confidence faltered. 'The crash came at the end of September, and was started by heavy selling in Paris which may have been at least partly due to politics,' continues Henry. The 1895 crash of speculative mining investments was not as serious as others preceding it. Violent rebellions against gold prospecting in Zimbabwe made investors more nervous, but the local impact of the financial chaos was contained. This was partly due to the Standard Bank's ability to protect itself by funnelling surpluses back to its London headquarters rather than investing them in Johannesburg.

Financial panic

*I*n the shakeout following the 1881 crash, the largest banks helped merge the diamond mines of the Rhodes and Barnato empires, sowing the seeds of monopoly mining capital. They also used the opportunity to drive away smaller financial competitors. Of 31 banks operating in 1862 – many poorly run and on the edge of solvency – only 11 remained in 1882.

But predictably, the supply of credit in the economy ballooned – and then burst again – just eight years later. Again the crash followed intense financial speculation, originating now from both Kimberley and the coastal financial centres of Cape Town and Port Elizabeth. And again the catalyst for speculation was the discovery of minerals – this time gold – and the issuance of all manner of charlatan mining company shares. Bank branch officers on the Rand were hopelessly out of touch with their head offices, according to accounts of the time, and they overfed the stock market beyond that which their balance sheets could bear.

'There can be no doubt that the banks, instead of exercising a steadying influence on business and speculation, had actually been instrumental in intensifying the expansion,' wrote Schumann. 'The result was that when the collapse came in 1889, the banks were again unnecessarily drastic in their curtailment of credit.' Gold shares were devalued by half in the process.

Seven out of South Africa's eight smaller district banks subsequently folded between 1890 and 1892, leading to even greater concentration in the financial sector and enticing fresh London finance – in the form of the African Banking Corporation – to the Cape and to the takeover of three of the failing banks. Standard continued to dominate the financial industry, and provided crucial help to Cecil Rhodes, not only in his governance of the Cape but also for the reach northwards into what eventually became Zimbabwe.

Financial power

The 'City' of London was not only the ultimate source of finance for mining, especially during speculative booms like 1895. It was also the headquarters of the Standard Bank and the Bank of Africa. And because of the links between the pound and the colonial currencies, the Bank of England was the *guarantor of the value of money* in South Africa, acting much as the Reserve Bank does today.

London financiers appeared capable of ruling the entire world at the turn of the century. But the Johannesburg and Kimberley allies of London bankers were also a force to be reckoned with. 'Nowhere in the world has there ever existed so concentrated a form of capitalism as that represented by the financial power of the mining houses of South Africa,' the famous economist John Hobson concluded at the turn of the century. 'And nowhere else does that power so completely realise and enforce the need of controlling politics.'

Kruger's Transvaal government responded to the big mining companies and the foreign financial threat by opening a local Pretoria bank in 1891. The National Bank of the Republic of South Africa supplied government and smaller Afrikaner mines and businesses with finance, and also issued government currency.

The National Bank served its monetary purpose even if, according to the Standard's JA Henry, 'speculation, extravagance and misdirected spending were very much in evidence, and the sudden access of abundant resources had tempted Kruger's government to adopt a policy of concessions and monopolies which antagonized the Cape and Natal without achieving its declared purpose of fostering local industries.'

The National Bank helped Kruger survive the financial instability and ill-fated Jameson Raid in 1895-96. However, following a binge of war-related currency printing and lending in 1899, the bank and the Transvaal currency became almost unsalvageable. After British forces invaded Pretoria in 1900, the bank's Afrikaner directors were all, save one, 'disqualified' by the British military governor. Yet the National Bank's noteworthy, if brief, impact on the Transvaal economy during the 1890s allowed Afrikaner national capitalism a temporary toe-hold. Three decades later, the Afrikaner response to the English-controlled economy was far more successful, resulting in what are today the Sanlam and Volkskas financial giants.

Race, capital and government

Despite Afrikaner suffering and bitterness, the Anglo-Boer War did bring recognition of their rights to self-determination. For example, the victorious British colonial government acted decisively to guarantee Afrikaner property rights against widespread seizures of land by blacks.

But deeper tensions remained, worsened by an economic slump from 1903-09. Although the economy was still dominated by white English-speakers, seeds were being planted for some dramatic changes, both at the level of economic control and in the way people (especially workers of opposite races) related to each other.

There was moderate prosperity from 1909 until World War I, a year-long slump, and then a five-year expansion based on substantial foreign demand for South African mining and agricultural exports. While the economy recovered, racial exploitation was officially intensified. It now extended far beyond feudal-style rural farming practices and mine labour into all walks of life.

After the 1910 unification of the Cape, Natal, Orange Free State and the Transvaal into the Union of South Africa, the central government was able to implement national-level policies relying on much more extensive administrative controls. Civil rights were now guaranteed for whites but not for Africans, coloureds or Indians.

Capitalist agriculture was a leading beneficiary, with increased government funding available to support land settlement, credit from the Land Bank beginning in 1912, marketing and irrigation. The 1913 Land Act, which stripped so many Africans of their traditional land and also prohibited squatting, climaxed a half century of intense economic conflict between white landlords and the African peasants whose surpluses were so important in meeting the food needs of the mining industry. The Act made only 8% of South African land available for Africans, later increased to 13%. This not only reduced competition for white capitalist farmers and supplied them with cheap labour but also, alongside agricultural mechanisation, increased the supply of blacks available for urban industry and the mines.

Small Afrikaner farmers were also hurt when rural capitalism forced them off the land, leading to the 'poor white problem' in the cities. While the manufacturing industry grew enormously in the Union's first decade, it relied on artisan production more than assembly-line workers. And skilled workers tended to be immigrants. Only big public works programmes in the 1930s and 1940s ultimately solved the poor white problem.

Manufacturing was becoming a crucial part of the economy. Food, beverages, clothing and building materials were prime areas of manufacturing in the 1800s. By 1910 the five leading industrial firms listed on the stock exchange were Pretoria Portland Cement, South African Milling, South African Breweries, Lion Match and Imperial Cold Storage. Total manufacturing output at the time was valued at about £17-million.

World War I sharply raised prices for many foreign manufactured goods. This prompted an increase in local production in key sectors like engineering and clothing in Johannesburg and shoes in Port Elizabeth. By 1921 manufacturing output had exploded to £98-million, and manufacturing firms employed 60 000 white and 110 000 black workers. The wage differential between these workers was nearly eight to one. As an African working class grew in the manufacturing economy, black urban family life developed.

African women appeared in the cities in greater numbers, but had access to menial jobs only. For those women forced to remain behind in the rural areas life was even harsher. They were undermined and exploited by the state, capitalist farming and by their men – at home and in the fields. This fall-back position may

The birth of Anglo American

The Anglo American Corporation of South Africa Limited (AAC) was founded in September 1917 by Ernest Oppenheimer, who was then 37 years old. This was the first opportunity for US capital to enter South Africa on a big scale. Oppenheimer withdrew his original name for the company – African American Corporation – as his main US associate felt it 'would suggest on this side our dark-skinned fellow countrymen and possibly result in ridicule.'

The original US directors included representatives of Newmont Mining and the extremely powerful JP Morgan banking empire. Future US president Herbert Hoover was instrumental in arranging the American side of the £1-million start-up capital. In addition to Oppenheimer, other founding directors were the National Bank chairman and the Union's first finance minister.

AAC chose a tough field to break into. Barnato Brothers, Consolidated Gold Fields and Central Mining/Rand Mines were all at least three times as large, even after AAC merged with the Mines Selection and Rand Selection companies.

But a year later the group realised a major coup – it acquired rights to Namibia's diamonds. The deal was based on Oppenheimer's government connections and JP Morgan's financing, and earned Oppenheimer a senior partnership in the London diamond syndicate. This allowed him to join Barnato Brothers in controlling the diamond trade the rest of the way up the West African coast. The two firms then ganged up on De Beers, and Oppenheimer claimed a seat on that powerful company's board in 1926.

A few years earlier, Oppenheimer was knighted in England and won a South Africa Party seat in parliament from Kimberley. This eventually proved useful, although the early years of his political career were spent with the opposition against an anti-mining government. His company was the only major mining house formally registered in South Africa, which he used to his advantage in dealing with National Party critics.

In 1929, Oppenheimer won the De Beers chairmanship through an audacious proposal to centralise the whole of the diamond trade. Through cross-holdings, AAC took control of both De Beers and the other main diamond company, Premier, and implemented Oppenheimer's vision of a full diamond cartel.

Oppenheimer's extraordinary rise to power was resented by many. During the worst months of the depression of the early 1930s, AAC announced massive production cutbacks and layoffs, apparently to prevent the price of diamonds from falling further.

'The fact is that the Hon. Member for Kimberley can juggle, manipulate and deal with all the diamonds he pleases,' scolded the Nationalist mining minister in parliament, whose constituents included white mineworkers. 'It is necessary for the government to take this great industry under its protection and that the interests of the public in general should not be lost sight of.'

But in March 1932 the diamond syndicate went ahead and shut down all deep-mine diamond production. Protests by some in government, and an attempted formal commission enquiry, were disregarded. Oppenheimer and the AAC turned their attention to gaining even loftier heights in the South African economy.

help explain why the peasant economy was preserved for so long under desperate conditions. In Afrikaner homes, young women had a much greater ability to escape enforced family sexism by moving to the cities.

Urban employers, especially in manufacturing, were guaranteed a stable and pliable labour supply because of the impoverishment of rural life, and they could also rely on laws like the 1911 Mines and Works Act and Black Labour Regulations Act to control black workers.

Racial wage differentiation and outright exploitation were even more extreme in the mining industry, where African workers were still largely migrant and faced declining real wages between 1910 and 1920. But there was increasing resistance, including forceful strikes at the end of the decade.

Skilled white mineworkers were rewarded with higher wages for intensifying the exploitation of the unskilled blacks they supervised. White workers also organised powerful trade unions that, in a series of intense struggles during the period following the 1907 depression, resisted efforts by mining capital to 'deskill' white workers hence rendering them replaceable by lower-skilled blacks.

These were not the only challenges to the commanding heights at the time. There was also turmoil in the banking system. Following a round of takeovers from 1910 to 1926, the number of banks was reduced from seven to just two big London banks and the smaller Netherlands Bank, headquartered in Amsterdam.

The period also saw a wide gap develop between the value of gold and the declining South African currency. This led to enormous gold smuggling from 1918-20. Ultimately, Union authorities decided this financial turbulence required a local guarantor for the banks and the currency. The Reserve Bank was founded in 1920, and put under direct ownership and control of private bankers – unlike other countries like Britain where government owned the central bank.

London financiers had become weak during World War I, and could not prevent this shift of power to South Africa. The big test of the Reserve Bank would be whether it could manage a real threat to South Africa's financial system.

The test came in 1926. With the National Bank ready to collapse, the Reserve Bank, supported by the Bank of England, arranged an emergency bail-out. The rescuing banks were the Anglo-Egyptian bank and the Colonial Bank. The merger of these two with National created Barclays – today called First National.

This was not the first time the young Union government would serve capital's most pressing needs, and would not be the last. Ever since, the South African Reserve Bank has been crucial in guaranteeing a friendly climate for banks, even when that has meant extremely painful interest rates for business and consumers.

A new alliance

Labour conflicts on the mines came to a head just when the economy began to stumble in the early 1920s. The Chamber of Mines went on an offensive against labour to offset rising production costs and a falling gold price. But white worker resistance became increasingly militant, culminating in the 'Rand Revolt' of 1922. The three-month mining strike led to a general strike and a brief armed insurrection in which 200 workers were killed.

The strike and the general social climate were made all the more fragile by the economic depression. The local depression began in the middle of 1920, closely following the world slump. It reached national proportions a year later, with gluts of products and massive unemployment in most towns. In 1921 consumer prices fell by 34% from the previous year, and imports dropped some 40%. Even luxury goods were hit hard – auto imports, for example, declined from 10 000 in 1920 to 2 000 in 1921.

The banks were, perhaps now by habit, easy to blame. Prime Minister Smuts accused them of having 'granted credit too easily and then curtailed it too drastically,' and after surveying the evidence CGW Schumann concluded that 'The indictment against the banks at the time that they became somewhat "hysterical" in their contraction of credit seems to be not unfounded.'

White farmers demanded a moratorium on loan foreclosures and a state bank. 'Government was even considering the appointment of district committees to intervene when debtors were unduly pressed, and to publicise the facts,' admits the Standard's JA Henry.

By 1923, South Africa had a bankruptcy rate 11 times worse than England and 34 times that of Scotland. In 1924 the Agricultural Credits Bill supported the introduction of rural credit societies, a stronger Land Bank, and a favoured position for farmers in their dealings with lenders.

There were ever-more striking class differences between white workers and rural Afrikaners on the one hand, and the foreign-oriented mining capitalists which had a large influence over the Union government on the other. The National Party, representing the Afrikaner petty bourgeoisie and farmers, and the Labour Party joined forces to form the Pact government which ruled for a decade from 1924. Official racism prospered, ensuring that all whites would have certain unalienable privileges.

The Pact cemented its social dictates with some crucial economic policy decisions. Tariffs were increased to protect local manufacturers, and extensive subsidies were granted, especially to agriculture. To pay for the programmes, mining capital was taxed heavily from 1927. The crown jewel was the establishment of the parastatal Iron and Steel Corporation of South Africa (Iscor) in 1928. With it a nationalist state capitalism arose distinct from English-speaking multinational capital.

'The prosperity of the undertaker in a plague'

As if to ignore new government programmes and subsidies, flows of private capital and credit again began to spin out of control. 'The larger centres in South Africa were overburdened with members of a trading and speculative class whose activities had a disproportionate influence on prices and prospects, but contributed very little to output and production,' says JA Henry about the mid-

1920s. 'This was beginning to look too much like an endemic weakness in the commercial community and in the social structure of the country.'

The year 1929 brought many tensions into sharp relief, in South Africa as elsewhere in the world. Local bankers were extremely eager to make loans, and land speculation meant that 'in some districts the value attributed to farm property looked to be 50% too high,' according to Henry. 'Standards had changed, and these were the days of the motor-car, bought for 30% of its cost in cash, and the rest on credit.'

There were also far too many agricultural goods produced for sale at a profit. The government responded by adopting more 'protectionist' policies. Imports of wheat, flour and sugar were discouraged, and a marketing board set up to support South African exports.

The other phenomenon of the late 1920s was enormous speculative fever in overseas stock markets – with the result that foreign investment in South Africa essentially dried up.

The 1929 crash initially crippled South Africa's diamond merchants. In panic, rich New Yorkers liquidated their personal assets and flattened diamond prices. Economic depression set in, and the demand and prices for most goods fell over the next several years.

Agricultural products bore the brunt of the collapse, despite government intervention on behalf of rural whites, especially laws supporting debtors' rights. By 1933, about half the country's two million whites could be classified as poor, 'not able to adequately feed or house their children,' according to one report. With many migrating from failed farms to cities, and sometimes living side-by-side with poor urban blacks, the poor white problem now posed a potential political threat to the government, which would have become more dangerous had the economy not improved.

In other countries the depression would last throughout the decade, but South Africa had an ace in gold. Although the formal international gold standard collapsed, the metal continued to play its traditional role as 'money of last resort.' Mine production set new records each year, and black labour was especially cheap and plentiful given unemployment elsewhere in the economy. But speculators were taking money out of South Africa because the currency, linked as it was to gold, was overvalued. After formally breaking from the gold standard in late 1932, South Africa's currency came back into line with its trading partners, and the economy began an amazing recovery. Gold, said a leading South African communist of the era, allowed the country 'the prosperity of the undertaker in a plague.'

With the mining houses now economically on top, their political interests stood a better chance of political success. Mining and financial capital gained access to state power through a coalition government in early 1933, as their South African Party 'fused' with the National Party.

The new Union Party combined 'maize and gold,' though some farmers and the rising Afrikaner petty bourgeoisie dissented. Aside from mining and agriculture, the rest of the economy had firmly revived by the late-1930s. The rebirth of gold spurred the growth of the engineering industry, supported by local iron and steel production.

Other big public works programmes – a third of which were financed by taxation of gold – continued to have a stimulating effect. Ventures included road building (1935), South African Airways (1935), South African Broadcasting Corporation (1936), and Agricultural Marketing Boards (1937).

Far-sighted manufacturers knew that a larger consumer market for their goods would be needed, and jobs were increasingly to be found on deskilled assembly lines. Indeed, many capitalists began publicly defending the use of black workers in industry against whites workers who saw blacks as competition. By 1939, South Africa could claim 800 000 black workers employed in manufacturing and mining.

In the course of tough organising by movements of squatters and homeless people, government authorities allowed relatively free access to the sprawling Soweto township during the 1930s and 1940s, and some Johannesburg city councillors were unable to win their repeated demand that the close-in township of Alexandra be 'removed.' While some progressive gains were won in the course of struggle, the *swart gevaar* panic that resulted from the integration of blacks into the workplace and cities played straight into the hands of the National Party which won the 1948 election with its pro-apartheid policy.

A white 'social contract'

World War II widened all sorts of social and economic rifts among white South Africans. The financial and mining elites were still loyal to London. Britain purchased the bulk of South Africa's gold and wool output during the war, and the government founded the Industrial Development Corporation to support new industries and boost old ones.

But there was initial uncertainty about how to manage the economy and construct a new social contract in the divided society.

The need for reconstruction was also based on fear of labour unrest. Unlike the changes of government in 1924 and 1934, the 1948 election was not the result of a national crisis of economic growth. The unions, claiming 40% of African industrial workers by 1945, had pressed for large wage increases throughout the 1940s and even pulled 100 000 workers from the mines in a 1946 strike. Black tenant farmers had demanded rights, and the Communist Party and African National Congress became increasingly militant and effective, even as state repression intensified.

The Smuts government could not guarantee the mines and farms an unlimited supply of labour. From fewer than 100 000 strike days per year in the early 1940s there were 1,4-million strike days lost during 1946. Severe repression returned peace to the shopfloor, and there were fewer than 50 000 strike days each year through the 1950s.

The other crucial split that affected the 1948 elections was ethnic, between whites in the ruling class. More than three decades after the Boer War, there was still a large current of opposition to Britain among Afrikaners.

At the start of World War II, the Afrikaner share of capital ownership was just 1% in mining, 3% in manufacturing, 5% in finance, and 8% in commerce, and a striking 85% in commercial agriculture.

A particularly sore point was the economic tension between the English-speaking financial elites and Afrikaner farmers. The former hammered away at the latter's state subsidies and at overproduction and land speculation problems, and advocated new farm taxes to limit mining's burden in bearing the brunt of government finance.

The economy was also changing direction. Between 1935 and 1945, manufacturing output galloped ahead of mining and agriculture, growing from £91-million to £265-million, and doubling again in the next seven years.

Mining output rose from £126-million to £192-million, and agriculture from £81-million to £164-million.

The end of the war aggravated rather than dissolved splits among whites. The Johannesburg stock market boom of 1946, for example, which doubled the number of companies listed, was far more beneficial to English-speakers than Afrikaners.

Eventually social and economic stresses ruptured the capitalist class to produce in 1948 a new ruling political coalition, organised by the National Party.

The opposition was Smuts' United Party, still representing English-speaking industrial and mining capital after 14 years of relative prosperity. Many capitalist farmers deserted the United Party, for very material reasons. 'The insistence of farmers on high prices and cheap labour,' comments the Standard Bank's Henry, 'seemed scarcely compatible with the

Apartheid cities

*B*lacks' movement to the cities did much to fuel white working-class racism in the 1948 election, and it also affected the development of the South African economy.

Even before mining compounds in Kimberley – where labour control and concern about theft were the apparent motives for segregation – there was evidence of racist social control by town administrators.

Nevertheless, black workers and merchants used to live in areas quite close to the central business districts of major South African cities (especially Johannesburg, Durban, Port Elizabeth and Pretoria). Cities were subsequently torn apart, as a result of an alliance between the white working class and big business, organised by the state.

This happened even before the Group Areas Act of 1950. In 1946, most land in Durban which is today industrially zoned, was zoned predominantly for black residential use. The local alliance already had its plan for the restructured apartheid city in place by 1943.

But, as we shall see, urban apartheid capitalism was not without its contradictions.

mining industry's need for labour and stores.'

The National Party appeared to offer Afrikaners their best employment hopes, through a system of 'state controlled private enterprise' which entailed a much greater dose of racism. Afrikaner *volkskapitalisme* combined more brutal control of black labour and high prices for farmers with government support for budding Afrikaner financiers (especially Volkskas and Sanlam), on top of increased national economic control. There was even a promise to nationalise the gold mining industry, leading to capital flight from the country in 1948 and 1949.

Following the elections significant sections of the business community accepted the broad social contract offered by the new government. Formal apartheid, they realised, could provide certain economic advantages.

Foreign funds

Economic growth in the 1950s and 1960s was based to a significant extent on new foreign investments, a fact which decisively affected the future of South African apartheid capitalism and resistance to it.

About 15% of the funding for new investments during the 1950s came from foreign banks and companies, especially in manufacturing. In many Third World countries this influence created overwhelming financial and technical dependence. But local control of South Africa's economy was supported by government policies which protected local industries from trade competition and also attracted skilled immigrant workers.

South Africa's ability to control foreign investment reflected the power of the mining houses, led by the giant Anglo American group. It avidly pursued local development opportunities – resisting funds transfers abroad – following the disruptions of global depression and world war.

The opening up of new mines in the Orange Free State placed enormous pressures on local resources. The entire infrastructure – from mines to new towns – had to be constructed, and costs for sinking shafts had trebled during the war. As a result, mining expansion over the period 1945-60 cost a massive £370-million.

The bulk of the funds – £160-million (43%) – was drawn from within the mining groups themselves. The windfall De Beers realised from sales of the diamonds accumulated during the 1930s helped Anglo marshal nearly £50-million for gold mining.

But more than a quarter of the money came from British financial institutions, mainly banks, insurance companies, pension funds, investment and trust units, and various other institutional investors. This reflected the rise of high finance within the British economy which, in spite of the global financial crisis of the early 1930s, culminated in their holding more than half of stock exchange shares by the mid-1950s. Another quarter of the mining industry funds was raised from mining trust funds in the US and Switzerland.

Following the partial 'delinking' of the 1930s and 1940s, South Africa's reintegration into international capitalism was complete, but the financing links would prove useful to anti-apartheid strategists some two decades later.

As new mining investments began to reap returns, local manufacturers began investing in the best technology that was increasingly available from overseas. Mining houses expanded into manufacturing, bringing along plenty of financing. And local 'money markets' sprang up to collect and centralise finance, and then place it where it realised the highest return. These markets were the turf of brand new financial institutions, largely set up by the big mining houses. Mines, banks and manufacturers were merging in a way that would affect the country's development through to the present.

US financial support

The expanding economy allowed workers greater bargaining power. Labour was weak following the severe repression of the late 1940s and as a result of the decline in bantustan agricultural capacity, which forced many more people into the cities. Once these areas served as 'reserve pools of labour,' but they soon became 'dumping grounds' for millions of African people who were displaced from 'black spots' in white areas of South Africa.

The ANC, South African Congress of Trade Unions and other organisations struggled to advance Freedom Charter demands during these years. But it was not until the shootings at Sharpeville and subsequent organisational bannings and life prison terms for ANC leaders in the early 1960s that resistance and repression made a serious impact on the South African economy.

For example, an extraordinary flight of capital from South Africa, amounting to R834-million between 1959-66, followed a net inflow of R134-million in 1958. The Sharpeville massacre woke the world up to apartheid, and sanctions lobbying began. One early target was the Chase Manhattan Bank, which, along with other US banks, stepped into the capital vacuum after Sharpeville with a $50-million government loan.

Ironically, Chase later precipitated the current financial squeeze when it created a capital vacuum in July 1985. And the sharp impact the disinvestment movement had on South Africa was due to the strong role US investment played in the early 1960s in propping up the apartheid economy when other foreign investors were fleeing.

Surprisingly, intense repression of black labour organisation in the early 1960s accompanied decent wage gains by black workers. By 1963 some stability had been re-established, and for a decade the South African economy grew at a rate of more than 5% each year (growth in the 1950s averaged 3,7%). Highly privileged white consumers formed the basis for much of the growth, as white wages outpaced inflation by a factor of three from 1948-73. The state imposed more import controls to support local production, and through massive borrowing continued to beef up its giant parastatal corporations. These in turn soon accounted for nearly half the manufacturing output in the entire economy.

Foreign capital – especially from the US – flooded back in the late 1960s.

Manufacturing profitability for multinational corporations, whose technology outran local competitors, was among the highest in the world.

As new foreign producers gained in influence, the character of the economy began changing. Foreign control of mining had decreased steadily, but both foreign manufacturing firms and financiers became much more important in the economy of the 1960s, the former accounting for a quarter of total output.

Men like American tycoon Charles Engelhard paved the way. With a background in minerals himself, Engelhard easily broke into South African mining, helped raise foreign funds for its expansion, and eventually became chair of Rand Mines. He raised $30-million in US investments for South Africa in 1963, and along with Anglo's Harry Oppenheimer, founded the pro-government South Africa Foundation. 'If you find somebody who doesn't like living in South Africa,' Engelhard once said, 'he hasn't been paid enough.'

Changes at the commanding heights

During the 1960s the geographical range of South African capitalism was enormously extended, and its economic power increased dramatically inside as well as outside the country.

Corporate control intensified as Anglo and the other major firms swallowed up hundreds of manufacturing, mining and agricultural companies. There was also a much larger role for Afrikaner businesses, largely through access to state patronage. Anglo American practically gave away the General Mining Corporation to Federale Mynbou (connected to the Afrikaner insurance giant Sanlam) in the mid-1960s, because of Harry Oppenheimer's desire to see the Nationalist government share material interests in the mineral industry with the English-speaking mining finance houses.

There was also very strong manufacturing and construction growth, and these sectors increased from 24% of the economy in 1962 to 28% in 1970, leaving mining and agriculture a smaller share (from 25 to 20% of GDP). The mining houses quickened their diversification into manufacturing.

Manufacturing production was changing. Under the increasing influence of foreign firms, new technology involved a transition from labour-intensive to capital-intensive production, especially in large companies. Enormous imports of sophisticated industrial machinery became an albatross around the South African economy's neck, leading to a foreign trade squeeze in the 1970s. Gold exports helped, covering deficits of around R48-million in 1964. But as the deficit grew to R1-billion in 1971, not even the soaring gold price of the 1970s could replace the shortfall.

As industry became more capital-intensive and internationally-oriented, a more sophisticated financial system was required. A 1964 banking law allowed banks and building societies greater depth and reach. Funds available to the banking sector spiraled, and financing on the Johannesburg Stock Exchange was boosted dramatically until a crash in 1969.

South African companies go international

In its own drive to go international, Anglo eventually came to own Charles Engelhard's firm, along with other foreign purchases during the 1960s. Anglo first went into Canadian mining, then in 1965 merged the London parents of Rhodes' old British South Africa Company, Consolidated Mines Selection, and Central Mining. By 1967, the company formed in the merger, Charter Consolidated, had operations extending across the globe and its value had doubled to £324-million.

This was small fry, though, compared to the stakes on the other side of the Atlantic. In 1970, following a partial nationalisation of the Zambian copper mines, Anglo's Zambian subsidiary was transferred to Bermuda. Renamed Minorco in 1974, the company soon became the largest single foreign investor in the United States, with more than $1,5-billion.

Ironically, Anglo's long-time chief executive, Harry Oppenheimer, was unable to visit the US for several years because the US Justice Department was investigating the extent to which De Beers' diamond cartel violated anti-trust law and hurt US companies. Oppenheimer's threat was, according to a 1974 memo of the Federal Bureau of Investigation, something akin to political bribery: 'The De Beers organisation is a large contributor to both political parties and should this investigation get to a stage where cases were actually filed we would probably receive much political pressure.'

His political connections gave the Anglo-De Beers chief enough clout to meet with John F Kennedy just after his victorious 1960 presidential election. Even so, the potential violations of US anti-trust law could have been so substantial that, remarked Oppenheimer after a 1976 US visit, 'I was just a little afraid they might throw me into a dungeon.'

Labour markets also changed during the 1960s, as South African miners went to work in factories, more immigrant mineworkers arrived, and farms were mechanised. There were a million manufacturing workers by the late 1960s, 400 000 workers in mining throughout the period, and around two million in agriculture.

The firms at the top prospered. Anglo's strategy for greater profits was shared, at least to some degree, by affiliates like De Beers, Rand Selection, Charter Consolidated, Rand Mines and JCI. Anglo came to control these firms not only through share holdings, but also through command over technological links and financing. And its industrial companies – which ranged over the entire spectrum of the economy – were characterised by their capacity to supply and consume products internally, within the 'conglomerate' structure, without having to pay a great deal of attention to competitors.

In sum, the 1960s saw a great deal of new investment, much of it from international sources, and much of it labour saving. The object of investment continued to be consumer goods, while production of machinery lagged behind. These developments played a key role in the economic crisis which began a few years later and from which South Africa has not yet emerged.

2

A crisis of over-accumulation

South Africa's economic slump has, since the mid-1970s, reduced the rate of economic growth per person to less than zero. The average South African has grown poorer over the past 15 years. Inflation has ravaged the currency, new investment in the manufacturing base has been slashed, and hundreds of thousands of jobs have disappeared. At the same time, billions of rands in profits have been made from financial speculation.

Some mainstream commentators have explained the slump in terms of the barriers that apartheid has placed on free market allocation of resources. They have also accused trade unions of demanding excessive wage increases at a time when worker productivity was slipping.

According to these economic analysts, the lack of new investment in productive equipment is largely the result of multinational corporate disinvestment and the absence of confidence in the country's political stability and future. Militant worker calls for sanctions and nationalisation have contributed to the slump, they claim.

On this argument, the economy would recover if apartheid ended, black workers were more reasonable and the international community again embraced South Africa.

But there are other explanations of the crisis, advanced by economists and social scientists rather more progressive than commentators from the mainstream.

The most thorough studies of South Africa's economic crisis are being conducted by the Congress of South African Trade Union's 'Economic Trends' research group. Many of the economists, assembled by Stephen Gelb, use 'regulation theory' to explain how a transition to a managed capitalism may be feasible through an African National Congress-Cosatu economic programme.

Other progressive theorists disagree with this approach, while still opposing mainstream explanations. Warwick University's Simon Clarke is a leading international critic of regulation theory, claiming that 'While this kind of analysis is fashionable in today's Sociology Departments, it has to be said that it is the most insufferable nonsense'. University of Natal economist Charles Meth is also suspicious of regulation theory, and is concerned 'to guard against conceding too much' to the apologists of capitalism.

Yet without question, Gelb is responsible for the most weighty radical economic analysis of South Africa in the past decade. The pathbreaking book he co-authored with John Saul in 1981, *The Crisis in South Africa*, focuses on consumer markets and labour conditions as reasons for the economic crisis: 'From the late 1960s, the growing saturation of the white consumer market limited not only sales but also the ability of the manufacturing industry to benefit from economies of scale. Since an expansion of the black consumer market was not then contemplated, this made more urgent the state's often reiterated, yet difficult to realise, call for an increase in manufacturing exports.'

In this explanation, insufficient demand for goods – or 'under-consumption' – is the cause of crisis. This is a fairly common argument, drawing on a mix of the British liberal economist John Maynard Keynes and the American Marxist Paul Sweezy. The implications are morally satisfying: give blacks more income, they will consume more, and that will spur the economy.

At first blush, this sounds logical both as a way to explain economic stagnation and as a possible solution. But does it really probe the roots of the way capitalism works? Marx argued that it 'is sheer tautology to say that crises are caused by the scarcity of effective consumption.' Charles Meth adds that '"Under-consumption", while always lurking, is not a theory of crisis, nor a permanent hindrance to capital accumulation.'

More recently, Gelb and many Cosatu economists have rejected the under-consumption argument. Gelb correctly predicts that if a post-apartheid government simply attempted a general redistribution of income from rich to poor, it 'would lead quickly to supply bottlenecks and higher levels of inflation, eroding any real gains. Furthermore, it would simply exacerbate one of the underlying causes of the crisis, which originated on the supply side of the South African economy.'

In other words, increasing the buying power of low-income blacks might fuel the economy for a short while, but would do nothing to solve the underlying problems.

A second explanation for the crisis focuses on labour. As white privilege became even more excessive during the 1960s, labour came under more intense pressure. This resulted in an explosion of strike activity in 1973.

On top of new-found labour militancy, Saul and Gelb also identify the shortage of skilled labour as a crucial weakness created by the apartheid system's colour bar and Bantu Education policies. These shortages became acute by the early 1970s.

According to this argument, economic crisis is rooted in worker resistance, leading to a 'squeeze' on corporate profits and a slow-down in growth. The implications of this argument will affect the labour movement's post-apartheid wage demands.

In a third explanation of economic crisis, Gelb's recent work goes beyond the consumer and labour explanations, and relates causes of the crisis more directly to capital accumulation. Increasing automation at the end of the boom (1970-73) ate away at profits, since automation shrinks the labour force which is the basis of exploitation and hence capitalist profitability. 'The growth of the capital-labour ratio accelerated, while productivity growth began to level off,' says Gelb.

Using this explanation, the 'solution' proposed for the slump is a new invest-ment programme directed by the state and aimed at producing mass consumption goods for a local market of low- and middle-income people. More labour-intensive production is the key to this programme.

This alternative investment programme is the centrepiece of the 'Growth through Redistribution' framework endorsed by the ANC and Cosatu at a May 1990 conference in Harare. But while based on profoundly progressive ideas, it is not clear that it will work under conditions of economic crisis.

Blaming the victims?

Gelb identifies rising wages as a key culprit – an 'originating cause' – of the crisis. The mid-1970s wage demands stemmed from increasing inflation – not the other way around – and from labour's increased clout in the wake of the 1973 Durban and PWV strikes. Wage increases in mining were also possible following the 1971 rise in the gold price. A second round of wage increases in the 1980s coincided with the massive consolidation of trade union organisation through the Federation of South African Trade Unions (Fosatu) and then Cosatu.

But this explanation for the economic slump is distasteful to some. As Meth puts it, 'There is a slight awkwardness about holding an analytical position which may be used to justify an attack on workers.'

Certainly, struggles between classes affect profitability, both on the shopfloor and in the negotiations over the distribution of corporate income between profits and wages. But those struggles cannot be the essential

Defining 'crisis'

Definitions are often crucial to the way a question is posed, and hence the answers that are supplied. One way to think about 'crisis', especially the current South African economic crisis, is as a 'turning point'. 'The popular connotation associated with "crisis"', according to Stephen Gelb, an economist at the University of Durban-Westville, 'is an idea of collapse or breakdown. But the original, more useful, meaning of the term is "turning point". In this sense a crisis of capitalism implies that the system cannot continue to develop along the same path as before – it must "adapt or die", as PW Botha eloquently expressed it more than a decade ago.'

But can South African capitalism easily 'adapt', or will some sort of major shock to the system be required? In defining crisis, Karl Marx talked of 'violent eruptions..., forcible solutions of the existing contradictions which for a time restore the disturbed equilibrium'.

The term crisis is best invoked, then, when problems arising logically from within a system cannot be resolved through the normal operation of that system. Some form of extraordinary intervention is required.

That intervention, as explained below, is 'devaluation of capital' which provides the 'forcible solution' and allows a new round of growth to begin. The task of this chapter is to explain how the South African economy has begun devaluation while attempting to withstand its worst effects in part through expansion of the financial system.

Regulation theory and 'racial fordism'

*T*he three radical explanations of crisis converge in what is popularly known as 'regulation theory'. This is a sophisticated variant of Marxism, developed in the 1970s in France, which examines the institutions and practices that develop over time in stable economies. Such economies are 'regulated': examples include the post-war combination of mass production and mass consumption in Europe and the US, called 'fordism' after Henry Ford, the automobile maker.

In South Africa the long period of growth that ended around 1974 was characterised by steady increases in automation and worker productivity. But the poorly-paid workers were black and the wealthy consumers were white, so Gelb coined the term 'racial fordism' to explain how the economy remained stable.

Manufacturing profits increased during the upturn of each business cycle. But as production increased, skilled labour shortages became acute, wages rose, and it became more difficult to import foreign machinery.

These bottlenecks relaxed when the business cycle hit a downturn. Production declined, and more foreign exchange became available for new investment. Unemployment rose, pressure on wages declined, and lower interest rates prevailed.

Gelb argues that 'The foreign exchange and skilled labour bottlenecks served to *maintain* the long term growth trend' because they prevented automation from increasing too rapidly.

Yet the stability provided by this arrangement could not last forever, and several factors combined in the early 1970s to change conditions drastically: increased labour militancy, international financial instability, and the rising cost of foreign machinery. Racial fordism had reached its limits.

This is a rich new way of thinking about the South African economy. But Simon Clarke's attack against international regulation theory must also be considered: 'This kind of analysis focuses on relatively superficial and transitory features of capitalism, which are one-sidedly elevated to defining features of a distinctive stage of capitalist development. The crisis is then seen only as a crisis of particular "modes of regulation" of capital accumulation, which can be resolved by developing new forms of regulation, rather than being seen as a crisis which expresses the contradictory form of accumulation itself. Theoretically this distracts attention from more fundamental and enduring features of capitalism. Politically it cuts us off from the lessons of history, and tends to validate opportunistic and divisive politics.'

reasons for capitalism falling into a long-term structural crisis. Normally, in fact, wages fall during a crisis. To paraphrase Meth, a profit squeeze arising from struggles over wages, while always possible, is not a theory of crisis, nor a permanent hindrance to capital accumulation.

If worker demands are seen to be a cause of economic crisis, there is a simple capitalist solution: 'wage restraint'. Gelb, for instance, cites 'a need to lower costs and improve productivity in the existing productive sectors, especially mining and manufacturing. This will require increased investment in new technologies, and/or lower wages at least in real terms. In other words, capital in these sectors needs to be strengthened, that is, profitability restored.'

But can such wage restraint resolve the crisis? The experiences of the US and Britain in the 1980s suggest not. There, highly distorted 'growth' was essentially 'borrowed' through massive debts and military spending, and substantially lower manufacturing wages did not contribute to any sort of longer-term economic solution.

Whether labour is targeted as a cause or not, the current crisis of capitalism is also self-inflicted. This is not merely a South African problem. At about the same time growth in South Africa slowed in the mid-1970s, the rest of the world economy (with a few minor exceptions) also began to falter. This world economic downturn is part of the story of South Africa's crisis.

International crisis

Tensions in the world economy stemmed in part from excessive US spending during the 1960s – conspicuous consumption, excessive overseas investments, capital flight to international financial markets, the Vietnam War, low taxes, and the slight strengthening of a notoriously weak social welfare programme.

But the US crisis was only the first in an international crisis of capitalism, which affected South Africa profoundly.

US president Richard Nixon, facing a re-election campaign, responded to the crisis in mid-1971 by defaulting on US obligations to sell its supply of gold for $35 per ounce. This $80-billion obligation arose from the 'Bretton Woods' agreement of 1944. Nixon's decision caused the gold price to soar. For a few years – 1972-75 and 1978-82 – the extraordinary price increases in gold helped South Africa counteract the long-term economic slump.

But from the early 1970s, advanced industrial countries passed on their inflation to South Africa through higher prices for imported machinery. Gelb has argued that the rising cost of foreign machinery was 'the primary initiating factor in the South African crisis', causing an inflation increase from 2,5% during the 1960s to more than 8% in the early 1970s.

Yet Meth argues that foreign machinery has never been that important to production. No more than 6% of manufacturing costs can be traced directly to foreign and local machinery combined. The exploding cost of raw materials, especially oil from mid-1973 on, is a better explanation for the transmission of the international economic crisis to South Africa. Following commodity inflation and two oil shocks during the 1970s, there was a massive global recession in the early 1980s and a general rise in the power of international finance. The shock waves hit South Africa hard in the mid-1980s.

What does this mean for the 1990s? If the international economic crisis was truly an 'initiating factor' for the South African crisis, that implies a need to delink from the world economy. After all, South Africa cannot expect to compete in a hostile international economic climate without importing even more high-tech machinery.

This matter may be resolved soon. If Pretoria and big business have their way, South Africa is likely to be pushed down exactly that economic path. Imported machines will be paid for by an enormous dose of foreign debt from the International Monetary Fund, the World Bank and large commercial banks.

Gelb and others in Cosatu's Economic Trends research group are aware of the problems of full-fledged export orientation and argue instead for economic growth through inward-oriented, labour-intensive investment. But if the problems lie deeper, even this progressive approach may not be enough to restart economic growth. Indeed if South Africa's current malaise began earlier – in the mid-1960s rather than the early 1970s – and if the problems were home-grown rather than imported, then a different picture of the economic crisis emerges, based on the problem of over-accumulation of capital.

Over-accumulation of capital

Whether inward or outward, labour-intensive or capital-intensive, the new South African economy will have a hard time overcoming the legacy of overproduction and excessive automation of the 1960s, which led to the decline in economic growth and the drought of new investment during the 1970s and 1980s. This 'over-accumulation' of capital best explains why South Africa's economy has become rotten with waste and speculation.

At the root of over-accumulation is the continual improvement of machinery and other productive forces. Too many goods are produced, workers are replaced by machines, and competition between capitalists becomes ruinous.

Over-accumulation leads to a situation in which goods cannot be brought to market profitably, leaving capital to pile up without being put back into new productive investment. Other symptoms include unused plant and equipment; huge gluts of unsold commodities; an unusually large number of unemployed workers; and the rise of speculation in shares and real estate.

When an economy reaches the stage of over-accumulation, it becomes difficult to bring together all these resources in a profitable way to meet social needs. Waste becomes the defining characteristic during a period of crisis. But this waste usually affects various parts of the economy in different ways. The most important symptom is an imbalance in investment between consumer goods production and production of heavy machinery.

From over-accumulation to devaluation

*C*apitalism is a system that must, to regenerate itself, creatively destroy over-accumulated capital, painful as this may be for the majority of people who are in the way. That process of destruction can be thought of as devaluation of capital.

Oxford University Professor David Harvey, one of the leading authorities on the topic of capitalist crisis, describes devaluation in the following terms: 'Capital can be devalued as money (through inflation or default on debts), as commodities (unsold inventories, sales below cost price, physical wastage), or as productive capacity (idle or under-utilised physical plant). The real income of labourers, their standard of living, security, and even life chances (life expectancy, infant mortality, etc) are seriously diminished, particularly for those thrown into the ranks of the unemployed. The physical and social infrastructures that serve as crucial supports to the circulation of capital and the reproduction of labour power, may also be neglected. Crises of devaluation send deep shock waves throughout all aspects of capitalist society.'

In the process, economic deadwood is cleared away, inefficient and outmoded companies are weeded out through collapse or takeover, large firms often get much bigger in the process, and labour is sharply disciplined as workers' living standards plummet. But it is also a time of extreme chaos at the pinnacle of the economy, giving poor and working people a chance to affect the outcome in sometimes substantial ways. This is examined in Chapter Four.

There are many examples of over-accumulation and devaluation throughout history. British historian Eric Hobsbawm identifies world capitalist crises lasting from 1815-48, 1873-96, 1917-48 and 1974 to the present. These are the endpoints of what are termed 'long waves'.

In South Africa, historian CGW Schumann identified 1881 and 1889-90 as the first real capitalist crises – financial crashes ripped the regional economy apart and devaluation was widespread in most sectors. Previously, crises had stemmed from natural disasters, crop failures, or political upheaval. The 1880s witnessed the first economic failures internal to South African capitalism.

Over-accumulation from the late 1910s to 1933 also cut big swathes through industry, finance, diamond mining and farming. This devaluation – followed by renewed demand for gold by a world economy suffering financial devaluation – set the stage for a new round of growth.

Are we now coming to the end of a long wave? And what sort of devaluation lies ahead? What will help to generate a new round of growth?

More control at the commanding heights

At the top of the South African private sector, Anglo American and its affiliates had acquired extraordinary economic power by the early 1970s. Overseas investments were increasingly successful. And locally, manufacturing and financial purchases were proving to be even more profitable than mining.

Some Anglo holdings – the South African Breweries and Safmarine conglomerates, for example – were clear cut. Others – such as the stake in Barlow Rand – were more complicated. What appeared on the surface as Barlow's 1971 takeover of Anglo-related mines, for example, actually represented Anglo's new control over Barlows.

In the financial industry, Anglo's merger and takeover successes were even more spectacular. Anglo's merchant banking subsidiary began a series of affiliations beginning in 1972 that gave it access to both Old Mutual and Nedbank. By 1974, Anglo had its own stake in the insurance industry, through a R160-million takeover of Schlesinger Insurance and Institutional Holdings, which in turn controlled African Eagle Life Assurance Society.

The Schlesinger takeover gave Anglo control over West Bank, which was then swapped for shares in Barclays National Bank. This ultimately led to Anglo's half-purchase of Barclays, followed by a full buyout at a deep discount, during the disinvestment wave of the mid-1980s.

In the meantime, Anglo's financial competitors were cutting their own deals. Sanlam entered an alliance with Volkskas and Trust Bank, and Pretoria began pressuring the big foreign-owned banks – Barclays, Standard and Nedbank – to be transferred to local control. Thus, Anglo and Old Mutual allied more strongly with Barclays, Standard and the Nedbank-UAL group.

By the mid-1970s the evolution of this process had 'transformed the face of South African finance capital,' commented Anglo-observer Duncan Innes. 'The financial oligarchy consolidates its power base; drawing new strength from production; gaining new sources of finance. No longer is the producer just a banker; now the producer-banker becomes the means through which a widening network of other producers and bankers can link up.'

Over-accumulation in South Africa

In 1978 Simon Clarke wrote: 'The economic crisis in South Africa is a manifestation of the failure to solve one of the perennial problems of South African capitalism, that of the relations between the different departments of social production'. He was referring to the economy's imbalance between investment in consumer goods and machines.

In the 1950s and 1960s an extensive range of consumer goods could be produced locally because the state provided generous protection from foreign competition. Import fees and tariffs amounted to 15% on consumer goods, compared to only 2% for imported machinery.

This captive market for First World goods attracted all kinds of foreign investors, who largely brought their own equipment with them. Much of it was top-of-the-line quality. Post-war growth in the South African economy was therefore based on excessive production of consumer goods, leading, in the 1960s, to over-accumulation in this sector.

The machines for local production of consumer goods were paid for with foreign exchange revenues earned from gold mining and agriculture.

According to regulation theory, this relationship between local manufacturing and gold exports provided enough balance to stabilise racial fordism. But the balance was already becoming undone – half a decade or more before the crisis really showed itself as a long-term decline in growth and investment in late 1974.

It is often difficult to tell exactly where an over-accumulation crisis begins, because capital and the state have so many avenues available to move the problems around without letting them bubble up to the surface. This was especially true in the 1970s, when the awesome economic power of the South African state increasingly supported what it perceived to be the long-term interests of South African capitalism, rather than just expanding Afrikaner employment rolls.

But there were unmistakable premonitions of crisis. The stunning crash of the Johannesburg Stock Exchange, from mid-1969 through 1971, was particularly telling. The big gainers in the two years before the collapse were real estate, banking and insurance, and mining finance. Of the industrial shares, commerce (including transport and services) rose highest and dropped fastest.

The feedback wounded some discount houses and commercial banks, and showed that South African markets were not all they were cracked up to be. Luckily for capital, though, the economy's 'fundamentals' were still reasonably strong, so the only serious losers this time around, it appeared, were investors in the new 'unit trusts'.

But the speculative financial markets were an indication that all was not well with the underlying economy. Just prior to the stock market boom, one of the most obvious signs of the impending over-accumulation crisis was the glut of private sector inventories – goods that could not immediately be sold and instead sat on shelves gathering dust. The five years leading to 1971 witnessed an unprecedented R2,8-billion worth of inventories piling up in the private sector.

This commodity glut was worst for wholesale trade, retail trade and catering establishments. Between 1967 and 1974, these companies accumulated R2,2-billion worth of inventories (at 1975 prices), while over the same period they put R3,2-billion into new investments. In contrast, the previous eight years (1959-66) saw inventories of just R453-million pile up in this part of the economy, as against a healthy and balanced R1,6-billion of investment. Thus, from 1959-66, the ratio of inventories to new investment was a reasonable 28%, but from 1967-74 it had jumped to an untenable 69%.

This glut of capital in consumer goods should have become apparent to observers well before the stock market surged and economic growth began to slump.

Over-accumulation worsens

Over-accumulation is always a potential feature of capitalism, but one that only becomes agonizing at key times when there appears to be no further profitable outlets for investment. In South Africa's case, over-accumulation exhibited itself first in wholesale and retail goods, next in financial speculation from 1967-69, and then became apparent throughout the economy.

By 1974, the bottlenecks first associated with the commodity gluts spread into other sectors. In manufacturing industries, new private sector investment in plant and equipment raced along until about 1973, leveled off, and then dropped significantly in 1976.

At that point, efforts to unload manufacturing inventories also began in earnest. What new private sector investment there was went mainly towards automation rather than opening new factories.

The essential dilemma was the continual drive of capitalism to overproduce relative to what could be sold. This quickly became obvious in specific manufacturing sectors. Local production reached certain limits to growth in the early 1970s. Some manufacturing sectors were affected much more than others, but the general response was more intense automation.

From 1970-73, companies automated at an astonishing 57% more-rapidly each year than during the 1960s. The automation growth rate from 1919 to 1976 was 1,5% per year, while in the 1970s automation increased by more than 4% every year.

As a result, private sector manufacturing jobs dipped dramatically, especially from 1975 on. 'The introduction of new technology meant changes in the imposition of the rule of capital at the point of production, on the one hand, and the creation of large scale redundancy, on the other,' according to Simon Clarke. 'During the boom of the 1960s economic expansion made it possible to keep the lid on the situation as employment opportunities expanded and some limited concessions could be made.' But not in the 1970s, as the Durban and PWV strikes were to prove.

Ironically, although the 1970s automation may have seemed to offer businesses

The geography of investment

*W*henever capitalism is in trouble, a frantic search for a 'spatial fix' begins. Manipulation of the economy's geography is a classic short-term response to a crisis of over-accumulation.

For example, declining private sector investment in South Africa since 1974 is closely linked to *international expansion* by Anglo American and other mining companies, Barlow Rand (grain), Liberty Life (British insurance), Rembrandt (international cigarettes), and the like. These companies were able to move substantial funds abroad or re-route funds from abroad. By 1980, more than R4,2-billion had been moved into direct foreign investments. By 1985, this figure had soared to R16,6-billion.

Pretoria's strategy was different, but also involved a spatial fix. Parastatal firms that classified as manufacturers – including Iscor and Sasol – undertook major building plans during the 1970s. Overall, their investments in plant and machinery increased to 17% annually from 1970-77, compared with 9% a year in the 1960s. To some degree this expansion paralleled the goals of the 1967 Physical Planning Act, an unsuccessful attempt to address the imbalance of investment in the PWV and other major economic centres.

More importantly, much of South Africa's 'built environment' – the entire range of factories, office buildings, residences and infrastructure that alter the natural landscape – was constructed during this time, so that at least temporarily investment and employment growth could be sustained during the 1970s.

But this was ultimately fruitless. As Oxford geographer David Harvey has argued, 'Each of the global crises of capitalism was in fact preceded by the massive movement of capital into long-term investment in the built environment as a kind of last-ditch hope for finding productive uses for rapidly over-accumulating capital.'

How 'massive' a movement of capital was there into the built environment, as the slowdown in productive investment began? During the crucial recessionary years of 1976-77, when business investment declined so drastically, hundreds of millions of rands that could have otherwise gone into new machinery made its way into outlets designed to overcome barriers to profitability presented by distance.

Some of the money went into better transportation. From 1970-77 the increases in annual investments in transport, storage and communication were 65% higher than the 1960s, even after inflation is discounted. Richards Bay was constructed during this period to lower transport costs for international trade. Iscor funded similar facilities – Sishen-Saldanha – to export iron ore. And South African Airways invested heavily in new aeroplanes, in part for its cargo trade.

Parastatals made huge investments in new electricity grids and water lines, for which the increases in annual spending from 1970-77 were 28% higher than during the 1960s. These also expanded the prospects for capitalist production and markets.

But while South African capitalists gained the benefits of the state's new spatial investments right away, the crisis in production itself was not overcome. Over-accumulation was not cured, and would bubble up again around 1982.

temporary relief through lower production costs, the basic economic crisis worsened. Industry after industry reached its limit. By 1975 the chemical industry stabilised at a point where it could produce about 85% of the total chemicals consumed in South Africa, but no more. In textiles and paper products, local manufacturing also hit the 85% barrier in the mid-1970s. South African-made rubber products had already stabilised at 80% of the local market.

The most serious barriers appeared in the motor vehicle industry, which moved quickly during the 1970s to occupy a stable 70% of the local market. But when that level was achieved, it was accompanied by near-ruinous overproduction.

The problem, argues Meth, is that 'when the phase of import substituting industrialisation came to an end and an export orientation was mooted (beginning in the early 1970s with the Reynders Commission), those capitals which had over-accumulated stood exposed. Not only can they not export profitably, but continuing protection is required as well for these high-cost producers, to prevent them from being eliminated by competition.'

Other basic sectors stagnated during the 1980s, finding no way to expand profitably. These included industrial chemicals, basic iron and steel, textiles and rubber products. None could find the means to increase their production capacity by more than 1% a year.

A few manufacturing industries escaped the worst effects of general over-accumulation, including beverages, paper and plastic products, food, tobacco and printing. New investment in these and several other industries was especially impressive during the brief economic upturn of the late 1980s, reflecting how worn out existing manufacturing equipment had become by that time.

But aside from mining, finance and a few other successful industries, it was becoming increasingly obvious by the mid- and late-1970s that South Africa was experiencing the beginnings of a long-term economic slump. Disruptions caused by intense township and shopfloor protests were becoming debilitating. Big business and the state were faced with a range of problems arising from the very structure of society.

Insiders and outsiders

With the crisis worsening, and political unrest a continual threat, a new 'social contract' was needed. In the late 1970s, the state began what Mike Morris of the University of Natal and Vishnu Padayachee of the University of Durban-Westville term a 'selective fordist' response to the crisis.

Based on the Riekert Commission findings, Pretoria launched a programme aimed at co-opting urban, middle- and some working-class blacks, while leaving the masses of poorer Africans in the bantustans. Riekert was supplemented by the Wiehahn Commission's legal recognition of trade unions, the Kleu Commission on industrial development and the De Kock Commission on monetary policy.

'They formed part of a market-oriented, monetarist state reform policy,' argue Morris and Padayachee. 'Capital and the state were starkly confronted with the realisation that their policy towards the popular classes had resulted in an overt unification along colour lines rather than a political division along class lines. This was very quickly recognised as a serious and dangerous problem.'

But the Riekert Commission's attempt to decentralise government responsibility to new black township councils only intensified black resentment and politicised more township residents. Other tactics followed during the 1980s: state-owned houses were privatised, the urban economy deregulated, and 'orderly' urbanisation allowed.

'The point was to encourage informal settlements for the poorest layers of the working class and thereby differentiate them from those layers of the working class which could afford ordinary, or upgraded, township housing,' Morris and Padayachee concluded. 'It (the Riekert strategy) proposes to use urbanisation to increase competition between workers, not only to hold wage levels down, but principally to act as a process of class differentiation. Those black workers who are unable to secure steady employment, secure housing and services are hence forced out of the more stable urban townships.'

For the 'insider' blacks, there would be a few more social benefits, ranging from education funding to electrification and township upgrading, collectively known by critics as the 'winning hearts and minds' strategy. Indian and coloured South Africans were also given a minor role in national policy through the tricameral constitution.

In its early days, the reform plan was endorsed quite emphatically by big business, and the opposition Progressive Federal Party faced serious desertions. But by the time of PW Botha's fateful Rubicon I speech in August 1985, most observers realised state reforms masked a deeper commitment to repression.

One result, after Botha's incompetent, scolding speech, was a complete collapse in

Political ideology at the commanding heights

*M*orris and Padayachee conducted a number of revealing interviews with business leaders, published in the journal *Transformation* during 1987. One leading official of a business association argued as follows:

'If ever there was a time for a dictator. Now a lot of people say PW is a dictator, but unfortunately he is a dictator within a democratic system, the parliamentary system. If he could have done away with that then it would have been a lot better.'

A senior executive in Barlow Rand agreed: 'We have to follow the path of the East Asian NICs. Study the economies of Taiwan, South Korea, Singapore, and Hong Kong. What is the government form in these countries? It is a dictatorship or colonial form.'

international economic confidence. The call for Botha to resign was made increasingly loudly in some business circles. Top business leaders made a quick trek to Lusaka to meet with the ANC the following month. Chris Ball, head of Barclays Bank, later left South Africa under pressure after financing an advertisement calling for the unbanning of the ANC.

Although Botha fumed about renegade business contacts with the ANC, organised capital – especially the Federated Chambers of Industry (FCI) and the Associated Chambers of Commerce (Assocom, now SA Chamber of Business) – kept close to Pretoria. In 1987 the important 'Corporate Forum' current within the FCI succeeded in purging its relatively activist chief executive, John van Zyl, because he was too critical of Botha.

The 1980s brought rewards for business. Pretoria adopted free market ideology with a passion and privatisation of major state-owned corporations provided a windfall of several billion rands to big corporate investors. The tax structure also changed dramatically during the decade. Corporations paid 22% of all taxes in 1980, and only 10% in 1990, while individual taxes rose from 20% to 34% of the total between 1980 and 1990. The new Value Added Tax also places the brunt of the tax burden on low-income consumers, this being consistent with recent trends in the most conservative countries.

Whether these and other big business windfalls undermine the effort to draw a small, privileged section of the working class into a new social contract remains to be seen.

Decentralising the problems

Regional policy in the 1980s was as flawed as other attempts to deal with South Africa's social and economic problems. 'Decentralisation', first seen in Verwoerd's large-scale forced removal schemes of the 1960s, then central to the 1975 National Physical Development Plan, received billions of rands in state funding during the 1980s.

The state's chosen growth points were mainly on the borders of bantustans. This allowed the state to combine its political goals with a manufacturing export strategy based on the familiar themes of cheap labour plus subsidies.

The bantustans themselves were getting a great deal more attention, with subsidies increasing from R90-million in 1970 to R1,4-billion in 1980 and R4,7-billion in 1985. State incentives to decentralised businesses included everything from rail, road and harbour transport subsidies, to inexpensive services, interest and wage bill subsidies, and tax relief. By 1990, 4 700 companies employing 200 000 workers had benefited from subsidies and the National Productivity Institute calculated that these enterprises generated nearly R10-billion in sales. Yet the decentralisation strategy failed, at least in terms of sprouting new, sustainable growth points in key areas.

The strategy also bred corruption, rapidly replaced male workers with females on the presumption that the latter are easier to control, and weakened urban trade

The Alexandra 'oil spot'

*T*he urban crisis has been one of South Africa's key flashpoints since 1976. Partly at the behest of big capital's Urban Foundation, PW Botha responded by granting the private sector a substantial role in proposed township development.

Johannesburg's Alexandra township is a prime example of the coincidence between Pretoria's and capital's views of reform. The impoverished township, surrounded by some of Johannesburg's wealthiest white suburbs, is home to an estimated 200 000 residents who are crammed into just 1,6 square kilometres.

From the 1930s onwards, these conditions bred extraordinary township resistance, featuring strong Communist Party and ANC influences. But the 1960s repression was successful, at least temporarily, in quelling revolt. When Planning Minister Piet Koornhof chose Alexandra as a model township for development in 1979, he was able to persuade a popular community organisation to join the town council. But development involved displacing many long-time residents so that new homes – vastly overpriced for most residents – could be built.

The reform strategy in Alexandra provoked enormous grassroots opposition during the first half of the 1980s, culminating in a 'six- day war' between the Alexandra Action Committee and the state in early 1986. Pretoria had by then dropped the reform mask, and viciously wiped out popular resistance – partly through use of murderous vigilantes and partly through a two-year treason trial of the township's top activists, in which they were eventually acquitted.

By September 1986 the government felt able to embark upon a winning hearts and minds campaign in Alexandra, spending R130-million on services and recreation. The plan included a new middle-class section of the township dotted with R50 000 homes: a 'five star lokasie', in the words of Alexandra resident Pascal Damoyi, 'meant for the town clerks, cops and teachers. The project aims to create a population of active, employed and skilled people, afraid of losing their expensive houses, tamed and effectively controlled.'

Big businesses chipped in, first on a charity basis, and then, by 1988, with construction for profit, housing development and financing. Landed and financial capital led the charge, and thus gave crucial support to Pretoria's extremely undemocratic reform strategy.

Organised resistance by what became the Alexandra Civic Organisation revived in 1989. As described in Chapter Four, the logical result of the earlier alignment of the state and big business is that Alexandra militants view business with great suspicion.

International finance to the rescue

*F*ritz Leutwiler, recently deceased, was 'a tough, no-nonsense character, with a fortuitous liking for South Africa,' in the words of *Leadership* magazine's Hugh Murray. Leutwiler once chaired the Bank for International Settlements, which is the central bank of all the international central banks. He was also chair of the Swiss National Bank when it gave South Africa financial support during the 1970s.

Who better to call on, in September 1985, to organise a bailout of South Africa, in the wake of overborrowing by local financiers and the harsh reaction of Chase Manhattan Bank? Leutwiler's story, told to Murray in early 1986, is revealing. 'Clearly the most significant pressure (on Chase and other US banks) came from important institutional customers who said simply that they would not do business with the banks unless they withdrew from South Africa,' Leutwiler testified. That pressure was in turn the result of US African-American activists, students, churches and even a few politicians heeding the liberation movement's call for sanctions and disinvestment.

Leutwiler explained that 'Officially the banks did not want to talk about politics, but they stated quite clearly when I met with them for the first time in London that they expected some positive political signals from Pretoria' before agreeing to a debt rescheduling deal.

During a trip to South Africa in January 1986, Leutwiler brought that message to the highest levels of government. 'I left knowing the signals would come. I said I needed something or I couldn't continue with my mission and be successful.'

The following month's rollover deal was a tough one for an economy in crisis, but it was certainly better than that imposed on most Third World countries. South Africa was forced to pay 5% of the debt immediately. The remainder was relent at a rate 1% higher than before. Similar deals – bailouts, but not on the best of terms for Pretoria – were made again in June 1987 and October 1989.

The financial freeze applied by Chase and other banks was, according to Stephen Gelb, 'possibly the one measure implemented thus far which could be said to have "worked," in this instance by forcing a major, though temporary, rethink amongst important elements of South African capitalism.'

Leutwiler was no friend of the ANC: 'My impression of the ANC is that it does not represent the blacks. I've had some experiences with communists, but to put it bluntly I'm reluctant to shake hands with a communist without counting my fingers afterwards.'

unions in sectors like textiles. Plant closings in South Africa's major cities coincided with new openings in decentralised zones.

Recently, because of sanctions and restricted access to Western markets, Taiwanese, Israeli and other decentralised firms have turned inward to compete with South Africa's big metropolitan firms, especially in garments, footwear and small electronics assembly. Thanks to the subsidies and much lower labour costs, the decentralised firms often come out ahead, and this has alienated the Urban Foundation, the Johannesburg Chamber of Commerce and the South African Chamber of Business.

The UF, which represents mainly metropolitan capital, is highly critical of state policy of marginal area development. In a policy document, the UF argued that 'Deconcentration points are unlikely to ever have facilities like zoos, opera houses, theatres, museums, large libraries, art galleries, landscaped parks, universities, technikons, private educational institutions, and so on'. 'It makes little sense to weaken the internal economic efficiency of the nation's "winner" region,' concluded the UF, referring to the PWV.

Decentralisation may indeed be one case where the state's response to the over-accumulation and political crises has not served the needs of those at the economy's helm.

Crisis in agriculture

It is a logical geographical jump from industrial areas in and near the bantustans to the country's white farms. There, even more than in the manufacturing economy, there is evidence of a severe crisis of over-accumulation.

Agricultural overproduction – in the case of maize, for example, sometimes twice the six million or so tonnes normally consumed – has, ironically, forced farmers to produce even more. This has been possible thanks to mechanisation and chemical fertilizers. The number of tractors in production increased by a factor of ten during the 1970s. Worse, they were paid for with enormous levels of debt (white farm debt is R15-billion today).

When drought hit and the land was mismanaged, the chickens came home to roost. By mid-1990, some 30% of the 80 000 white farmers faced insolvency. This time Pretoria could not jump in with assistance. In 1970 subsidies amounted to 20% of farm income, but today a bailout of failing farmers is almost impossible. Indeed, the state is cutting back on farm subsidies, an action which has resulted in a huge swelling of the ranks of the Conservative Party. Farming has largely fallen into the hands of corporations and large-scale farmers, with most farms now more than 1 000 hectares in size.

Pesticides helped increase large farm output dramatically, but at great expense to the health and employment of farmworkers and their families – as many as six million people. These people are probably South Africa's most impoverished and helpless workers. Many live under slave-like conditions, tied to their employers by personal debt and a total lack of alternatives. Women and children, together with many illegal foreign workers, make up a large percentage of these labourers.

In addition, agricultural mechanisation during the past two decades forced hundreds of thousands of people off white farms into hostile cities or barren, overpopulated bantustan areas. Previously farmworkers had some protection through the labour tenancy system, having access to small plots of land to produce for their own needs. But capitalist wage relations have since stripped farmworkers of even that slight level of self-sufficiency.

From monetarism to financial explosion

Perhaps the most damaging feature of the economy in the 1980s was the extremely high rate of interest – the cost of money. Marx once noted that, in times of crisis, 'the demand for loan capital, and with it the interest rate reaches its maximum; the rate of profit as good as disappears, and with it the demand for industrial capital.'

Ironically, the demand for 'loan capital' (credit) rose dramatically in the 1980s, during exactly those years when interest rates peaked. South African banks once limited the amount of their outstanding private sector loans to around 30% of annual economic output. But in 1980 that figure began rising steadily, reaching nearly 50% a decade later.

After taking inflation into account, interest rates were at a very low –6% in 1980. It was a good time to borrow. But the low interest rate lasted only briefly. With international financial pressure, South African interest rates soared to 12% (after inflation) over the next four years. Banking and finance had become, by early 1985, the most dynamic sector of the economy.

Across the globe, bankers strongly exercised their power over governments throughout the 1980s. In the US in 1979, a Chase Manhattan banker, Paul Volcker, was appointed to chair the Federal Reserve Board, replacing an industrialist perceived to be too weak to cure rampant inflation and the declining dollar. In September that year, at the annual IMF/World Bank meetings, international bankers informed Volcker in no uncertain terms that he had to do something drastic to rescue the dollar and attract money back to the US.

Volcker returned to Washington and tripled US interest rates, in the process bringing on the worst economic slump since the 1930s and costing President Jimmy Carter the 1980 presidential election. This was 'monetarism', for it involved reducing the amount of money in circulation. As a theory it was also applied elsewhere in the West, including Britain in 1976, when the IMF dictated economic policy to the Labour Party. The impact of such financial power on the Third World was enormous: the worst debt crisis in world history.

Government policy in South Africa, Vishnu Padayachee and Mike Morris concluded, 'was buttressed by the international ascendancy of monetarism and of finance capital. The domination of international economic affairs by developments in the international capital markets from the late 1970s bear testimony to this. In South Africa, local finance capital appeared to have a lot to do with shaping the local monetarist initiative, including the removal of interest rate ceilings and foreign exchange controls.' As those controls slackened, at least one short-sighted response by South African companies was to borrow from foreign banks. Foreign money was cheaper, and while South African interest rates rose, international interest rates were dropping.

From 1983 through mid-1985, South Africa's biggest banks went to international credit markets on behalf of their corporate clients. The economy was in the throes of recession, new productive investment had halved from R7-billion a year to R3,5-billion, and profits were simply much easier to be had from playing the financial markets.

A leading US Marxist, Paul Sweezy, calls this situation 'the financial explosion'. Indeed, it soon became an extremely risky proposition. The borrowings were short term, and required friendly bankers to 'roll over' (reschedule) the lines of credit from time to time.

In July 1985, Chase Manhattan Bank, formerly an important backer of South Africa, decided that the economic and political situation had deteriorated too much. Chase pulled the plug, terminating a $500-million short-term line of credit. Numerous other US banks followed. The consequences reverberated far and wide across the economy and politics. The ANC's use of this opportunity and its strategy for further financial sanctions will be taken up in Chapter Four.

Speculation vs investment

The 1980s were a period of drought for new productive investment in South Africa. Manufacturing capital stock (plant and equipment) peaked in 1984 at around R50-billion and, when inflation is taken into account, has been declining ever since. Employment in manufacturing also declined, since the little new investment there was made production relatively more capital-intensive.

The problem was not, as many mainstream economists argued, lack of savings in the economy. Savings or not, the banking system found ways to create record amounts of credit each year. Corporate savings actually increased from a low point in 1982 to 1990. But the savings did not translate into investment in productive plant and equipment.

In South Africa, corporate savings are rarely used – as they should be – to plan for new investment or as a nest-egg to guard against unforeseen problems. Instead, they make their way into high finance. In the money markets, the rate of return is much higher than corporations receive from new productive investments. Personal savings (much reduced in recent years as incomes dropped) are mainly captured by insurance and pension funds, which are pumped largely into speculative outlets. A trade union guide to pension fund investment returns during the 1980s listed the best earners as unit trusts (23,6% annual return), JSE financial and industrial shares (21%), and property (16,6%). The inflation rate during these years averaged 14,5%. The high rate of return on the JSE meant that the value of shares rose from around R50-billion in 1982, following the gold slump, to nearly R400-billion in

1990. And real estate transactions doubled from around R10-billion a year in the mid-1980s to R20-billion in the late 1980s.

The JSE is absurdly speculative; its mission is accurately described by ANC economists as 'paper chasing paper'. South Africa's largest company, Anglo American, controls anywhere from 33% (Anglo estimate) to 45% (independent estimate) of the JSE, while Anglo and the next five firms account for 80% control of the stock market.

The paper value of JSE shares has risen dramatically over the years in spite of the very small volume of shares traded (just 5% a year, compared with 50% or more in many major stock markets). This has allowed a few major players to tinker with share values almost at will. In 1989 the JSE rose by 50% in US dollar terms, the highest increase of the world's major stock markets. And again in 1990, the JSE rose fastest, in terms of local currency (Hong Kong was slightly higher in US dollar terms), even though the economy was shrinking rapidly.

During the 1980s then, over-accumulated capital was placed in the JSE, real estate, and various other financial markets, rather than in new productive plant and equipment. This also happened globally, with particularly dangerous side effects as international financial markets began coming apart at the seams in 1990.

Disinvestment: A red herring?

Apologists for South African capitalism often claim that sanctions were the main cause of the poor showing of the economy and the investment drought, especially since 1982. Disinvestment and sanctions have indeed hurt the economy – perhaps by as much as R40-billion according to Cosatu, but this may be a short-sighted measurement.

The fact that disinvestment has allowed local firms to purchase multinational corporate assets at a deep discount means that the South African economy is that much more locally-controlled.

Yet the downside of sanctions cannot be discounted. The firms that left were often those with the strongest corporate conscience – borne of intense popular pressure in their home countries – and many workers suffered during the process. The new owners were usually less committed to union rights, company desegregation and the social investments encouraged by the 'Sullivan Principles' and European Economic Community codes of conduct.

Sanctions forced an 'inward industrialisation' programme in the late 1980s that, along with tough import controls, spurred some new investment. That programme, we shall see in Chapter Three, has been replaced by a new export-oriented growth strategy which, according to some in the ANC and Cosatu, poses new dangers.

This review of the South African economy has provided some rather striking conclusions:
◆ the conglomerates at the commanding heights of the economy – more so than workers or international influences – have, since the late 1960s, been at the centre

Disinvestment, De Beers
and the Soviets

Disinvestment by South African firms had a lot to do with the 1980s investment malaise. It is ironic, given the claims about sanctions damaging the economy made by South Africa's elites, that there were few objections to what may be the largest disinvestment of South African capital, announced by De Beers in 1990.

In early 1990, as the euphoria surrounding the release of Nelson Mandela cooled and international investors pulled back from the JSE on alleged fears of nationalisation, De Beers cemented the 'chicken run' mentality by moving its foreign business operations to Switzerland. These operations, accounting for some 80% of its profits, revolve around the Central Selling Organisation diamond marketing agency and De Beers' interests in Botswana, Namibia and various overseas firms.

De Beers went on, in July, to grant a $1-billion loan to the USSR as part of a $5-billion diamond cartel arrangement. The loan – secured by diamonds – gives the Central Selling Organisation full rights to market Soviet diamonds for five years.

This deal, which the *Financial Mail* described as 'sweet, necessary and full of promise,' is out of character with the USSR's historical commitment to the liberation struggle, and its economic background is important. The USSR's $80-billion foreign debt was trading at a deep discount in financial markets. 'The spectre of a Russian debt moratorium cannot be ignored,' announced the *Sunday Times* finance pages in early June. 'It is quite possibly the reason behind the trade negotiations that SA has been conducting with Poland and Hungary.'

At about that time, the USSR proposed the diamond deal to De Beers. 'Our breath was taken away,' says Gary Ralfe, the De Beers director who cut the deal. 'It's a huge sum in anybody's books.' It is also a huge stake for South African multinational capital in a country that once offered the strongest support to the ANC and its armed struggle.

of the problem of over-accumulation and hence the current economic crisis;

◆ investment by parastatal corporations and new economic strategies (tax cuts, privatisation, deregulation, 'winning hearts and minds') were used by Pretoria to support big private firms, but in the end failed to solve the underlying crisis; and

◆ the most recent responses of corporate elites – including international capital flight, rising levels of debt in the economy, and unprecedented stock market speculation – will hamstring any reformist economic policy for years to come.

Since 2 February 1990, policy-makers – from right and left – have been paddling into the turbulent economic waters of over-accumulation. Worse, the hazardous currents of devaluation are appearing on the horizon.

Big business is relatively accustomed to staying afloat under these conditions – though for how much longer this is possible is not clear. Some business leaders have persuaded the ANC to accept very conservative lessons in managing a sinking ship. But the ANC's own programme may still stand a chance of moving some third class passengers up from the bilge and pushing some white males away from the helm. The next chapter tells the story of this contest.

What the previous pages make clear, however, is that the South African economic ship always was, and still is, a slaver, and will probably remain so into the 1990s. If it runs aground as a result of worsening economic crisis, it is heartening to note that the oppressed have already begun constructing their own life boats, in ways that are considered in Chapter Four.

3

'Solutions' to the crisis

A new South African government, based on one-person-one vote in a unitary state, will probably be elected before the century ends. That government – almost certainly including the African National Congress – will have outlined some basic economic principles ahead of time.

This chapter looks at the pressures on the ANC to develop a 'realistic' economic policy in this run-up to a transfer of power. Big business is pushing the ANC to compromise on crucial questions of property rights, international relations, monetary policy and the orientation of state subsidies. By late 1990, big business was celebrating a victory over at least the changed economic rhetoric of the ANC. Other more tangible gains – an end to sanctions, prospects for new foreign investment and huge foreign loans – were within sight.

In a highly symbolic move made in Geneva during October 1990, the ANC's Thabo Mbeki joined Finance Minister Barend du Plessis in a united front, attempting to attract foreign corporations to a post-apartheid South Africa. A good business climate was promised. These words may sound as ominous to workers here as they do to others across the globe, all tightly trapped in an international economy where wages, safety, health and environmental standards have sunk to pitifully low levels.

An alternative strategy – which progressive ANC and Cosatu economists term 'Growth through Redistribution' – offers greater hope for the majority. This is directly opposed to the programme of big business, and only time will tell whether its adherents are strong enough to have it adopted as official policy.

Yet even this exciting and humane approach is based on a restricted view of the economic crisis (regulation theory), and if implemented in the 1990s might run up against the constraints of over-accumulation and devaluation.

What does big business want from the ANC?

South Africa's economic crisis could not have come at both a better and a worse time for the African National Congress.

The crisis intensified at the same time as several important political factors came into play. This may make a crucial difference in the speed of transition to democracy and the possibility of progressive reconstruction.

Labour and community resistance were central to the political crisis. The rise of unions and the black consciousness movement in the early 1970s, followed by the Soweto uprising in 1976 and the successes of broad popular front organisations in the 1980s all played their part.

International solidarity movements were reinvigorated after the 1984 community protests in the Vaal Triangle reminded the world of the need to confront Pretoria. And as the broader global economic crisis swept through the Eastern Bloc, stripping the Soviet Union of its capacity to underwrite the ANC, the geopolitical stakes favouring South Africa's rulers were permanently lowered.

Enlightened business leaders recognised the potential for this moment a couple of decades ago. Then and now they knew that if change ensures some social stability, allows shopfloor control to become less politicised, eases rigidities in labour markets, limits apartheid's many other costly geographic irrationalities, and opens the door to international markets, it can serve capitalist interests well.

But will this sort of transition rekindle economic growth? And what would be the costs to an ANC government unable to allocate resources to its constituents in line with the promises of the Freedom Charter?

The economic crisis helped place the ANC within reach of state power. But the reigns of government in the 1990s will be slippery if the economy continues to stagnate, if speculation is not cured, if wages are put under pressure, if poverty in urban and rural areas intensifies, if AIDS reaches uncontrollable levels, and if international economic conditions weigh down South Africa.

Can the ANC and its allies construct an economic programme that would counteract these dangers? And what do the state and big business have in mind for economic restructuring? Do they want to use the ANC as little more than a front?

This scenario is already being planned by a group political commentator Mark Swilling has termed the 'econocrats'. Some trade union and community activists term this the 'sell-out' solution.

Whether it is the route ANC leaders will tread to gain the political edge in final constitutional negotiations remains to be seen. But the broad direction of this route can be identified ahead of time.

Sell-out?

Business Day comments: 'With the rise of Barend du Plessis, the Finance Ministry was no longer overshadowed by the Botha securocrats. The Reserve Bank under Chris Stals was likewise calling the shots. Sound economic policies replaced haphazard strategies designed to win white votes.' The 'securocrats' – those government officials whose speciality in the mid-1980s was military and police repression – were out of favour.

The econocrats, Swilling says, rose to prominence alongside FW de Klerk, and serve as the brains informing economic policy. 'They're urban policy planners of big capital in the Urban Foundation (UF), liberal economic reformers in the Development Bank of Southern Africa, and state officials.' He has argued that econocrat policy ideas 'are probably the most important component of the liberalisation phase that will precede the democratisation process.'

This liberalisation involves re-channelling tens of billions of rands – both publicly and privately controlled – in new directions, and is reshaping the battle-fields on which many political struggles will be waged in the 1990s.

According to the Urban Foundation, for example, 'The R2-billion set aside in the 1990 budget for a development trust to be headed by former UF chairman Mr Jan Steyn could have a vital impact on city development – and on city politics.' The Steyn Fund, argues the UF, 'could create a climate more favourable to constitutional talks.'

The econocrats are trying hard to win the ANC over to their view of development. Left-wing critics in the unions and small Trotskyist formations like Workers Organisation for Socialist Action and New Unity Movement believe deals may already have been cut in private meetings between big business and ANC negotiators. They point to press reports of the ANC on the doorstep of huge corporations, asking for handouts in the form of seven-figure charitable contributions.

Private meetings and requests for donations do not necessarily imply a 'sell-out'. But the ANC does seem to have less and less political and economic room for manoeuvre in its dealings with both big business and the state. Already significant ANC concessions on armed struggle, nationalisation and intensified international sanctions have limited the scope of the next round of struggle.

Pretoria initially responded to ANC offers with friendly gestures and the promise of more talks. But its response also included a brutal backlash that led to unprecedented violence. As the destabilisation tactics of state securocrats hit home (with and without the participation of Inkatha), the ANC grew weaker and less confident.

Earlier, in the winter of 1990, JCI economist Ronnie Bethlehem had advocated state spending of R20-billion over three years on housing for low-income blacks. Nedbank executive Merton Dagut and the NP's influential Glenn Babb both suggested economic 'reparation' for the sins of apartheid was in order.

But as the limits of ANC strength and organisational capacity became clear during the Reef bloodshed, influential economic figures felt less bound to treat the ANC with respect.

At the same time, pro-business Chief Gatsha Buthelezi is still well favoured by the top business leaders who lifted him to international prominence. Even during the worst of the killings in July, August and September 1990, and where Inkatha members were alleged to be directly involved, he received not a word of corporate condemnation.

Some in the ANC argue that it is these businesspeople who must be brought on board the democratic alliance during these crucial months prior to liberation. Many in the left of the movement, however, ask whether the capitalists have earned this place.

The econocrats' three myths

1. To grow, South Africa must be tied closer to the world economy.
Historical evidence suggests otherwise. South Africa's most robust growth occurred between 1936 and 1951, when, due to the Great Depression and World War II, international economic relations were at their weakest in modern times.

During this period, productive investment was very strong. Plant and machinery growth, at 8% annually, far outpaced any other period (the 1919-76 average yearly investment growth was 5,9%, and it has been much lower since.) And from 1936-51, employment grew by 6,2% a year (1919-76: 4,4%).

Production was relatively labour-intensive, and increases in worker productivity low. But the black wage share rose from 11% to 17% of total wages during this period, the best increase in the country's history. By 1976, the black share of wages was still just 20%.

This evidence corresponds to the general argument made by Andre Gunder Frank, the founder of 'dependency theory'. Frank insisted that, for some countries on the periphery of the world economy, a stronger, more balanced, and locally-controlled economy can only develop by lessening international economic ties.

If an ANC-led government directed the economy towards relatively labour-intensive production of low-tech, low-cost consumer goods, as promised in the Growth through Redistribution programme, there might be no need for tighter connections to the world economy.

2. There is not enough money in South Africa to support grandiose social programmes. Foreign loans and investment are therefore essential.
The Johannesburg Stock Exchange attracts billions of rands that could go into productive investments. Indeed, hundreds of billions of rands were misallocated in this fashion during the 1970s and 1980s, through over-accumulation.

As a result, control of resources by financial fund managers is so fickle and irrational that on just two days in September 1990, nearly R30-billion was shed from the JSE during a market crash.

Had it been invested instead, that R30-billion could have provided – twice over – electrification for the 70% of South Africans who have no supply.

3. *Spending heavily on social programmes will fuel inflation, which is an economic cancer.*

Inflation has complex roots. On the one hand, monopoly companies control key industries, and are able to set prices at inflationary levels. By the late 1970s, three or fewer companies controlled breweries, cigarettes and tobacco, pasta, coffins, fertilizers, matches, printing, glassware, engines, tractors, office machinery, batteries, motorcycles, aircraft, and watches and clocks.

On the other hand, loose credit policies and the deregulation of the financial industry are also to blame. As Nedbank chief economist Edward Osborn admits, 'We've had a massive, exponential rise in financial flows which are just swirling about, going into an inflation of values, financial assets, feeding a whole inflationary process in this country.'

This problem – inflation as devaluation of money – does not presents itself only as a constraint on economic restructuring, *but also as an opportunity*. Inflation involves redistributing wealth from bankers to borrowers, which is why financiers hate it so much. Inflation means money borrowed yesterday is worth less when paid back tomorrow.

Under most circumstances inflation hurts financiers, even though they contribute to the problem through their easy credit policies. But in the late 1980s and into the 1990s, inflation did not present a major problem to the banks because the rate of interest was higher than the rate of inflation.

With lower interest rates, a social welfare programme could be financed by printing more currency, and by ending the tax incentive for borrowing.

As ever, the issue is whose interests are being served. Financial elites did very well from high interest rates in the 1980s. However, inflation could also be a tool for the gradual redistribution of wealth in the other direction.

Housing finance oils the wheels of township capitalism

Among the most visionary of the new breed of econocrats is Charles Simkins, a University of the Witwatersrand professor closely associated with the Urban Foundation. Simkins says South Africa's economic future depends in part on 'the penetration of market relations into black housing', involving new housing finance schemes co-ordinated through the private sector.

Simkins, the UF and the Association of Mortgage Lenders devised a housing finance scheme in 1989 which is expected to increase the flow of money into black housing by at least R1-billion per year. (By the late 1980s building societies and banks had made R5-billion available to blacks for housing bonds.)

This scheme, the Loan Guarantee Fund, makes housing bonds averaging R25 000 profitable to lenders through some tricky accounting and a general rise in banking risk levels.

The attempt to initiate home-ownership in communities which for decades have rented housing from the state is a profoundly political act. As Democratic Party leader Zach de Beer put it: 'When people are housed – more especially when they are home-owners – they are not only less likely to be troublesome, they are also likely to feel they have a stake in the society and an interest in its stability.'

For some financiers, the Loan Guarantee Fund represents a crucial chance to expand. In mid-1990, amidst reports of record levels of consumer indebtedness and repossessions, Bob Tucker, managing director of the Perm, told a conference of estate agents that 'the capacity to borrow further has for most people now reached the ceiling.' Existing markets are drying up but the untapped black market looms as an option. The scheme, therefore, targets the privileged portion of the working class – hundreds of thousands of homes which can be used as collateral for both a housing bond and a large dose of consumer credit.

Driven to export?

According to Finance Minister Du Plessis, South Africa aims to 'export as never before.' This is the most crucial element of the econocrats' programme. But it is not certain that an export strategy will work.

It is true that South Africa has managed to increase exports in recent years, in spite of international sanctions. There was a desperate need for foreign currency due to the debt crisis. Fortunately for Pretoria, sanctions loopholes and new Asian markets permitted the expansion of exported coal, uranium, platinum, paper pulp, iron and steel, ferro-alloys, copper, nickel and diamonds.

But whenever international recession hits, raw material exports suffer most. By the time FW de Klerk became state president in 1989, the end of the 1980s global economic upswing was in sight. Government and big business agreed that a move to *manufactured* exports – not just minerals and agriculture – was essential for future growth, and subsidies were made available for this purpose. For example, in September 1990, Eskom granted 40% rate discounts to clients who export goods, while simultaneously forcing local authorities to cut electricity to dozens of black townships which were in arrears on payments.

Export incentives cost the taxpayer around R1-billion each year. Pretoria's South African Foreign Trade Association (Safto) directs this money, and in the 1990s hopes to support export of products like chemicals, paper and packaging, processed foodstuffs, automotive and transport equipment and engineering technology.

The export push will be not be easy. Adding more local value to mineral exports – 'beneficiation' – is not impossible. But officials of the South African Production and Inventory Control Society have admitted that 'the quality of South African products and services is among the worst in the world.' Yet Safto somehow believes local producers, long protected by import barriers, will soon be able to compete with export 'tigers' in South Korea, Hong Kong, Malaysia, Thailand, Singapore and Taiwan.

The rest of the agenda

The econocrats' economic programme may focus on exports, but it includes a number of other aspects:

◆ *Deregulation of commerce and liberalisation of South Africa's financial markets will continue.* This will allow capital to flow more rapidly beyond any governmental or local system of control. Subcontracting and self-employment will be encouraged, and some small businesses will have special rights to avoid minimum wages and provisions protecting health, safety and building standards.

◆ *Further privatisation of state assets is on the cards.* The November 1989 listing of Iscor on the JSE was a success for the state and big business. Privatisation allowed initial investors – mainly the large conglomerates and finance houses – to reap a tremendous windfall when Iscor share prices immediately soared. But for

Capital flight, AIDS and counter trade

*T*he odds are against South Africa surviving the rigours of international competition in manufacturing. Despite this, the export strategy is strongly favoured by many.

One reason may be that business is looking for easier transfers of money to international safe havens, and this happens much more easily under free trade policies. Under the present exchange control system, the Reserve Bank is investigating dozens of foreign exchange fraud cases simultaneously. In 1990 some cases involved respectable institutions and huge sums of money: Repfin (R350-million), Trust Bank (R187-million), Eskom (R170-million), Sterns (R170-million), Vermaas (R150-million) and many others.

The scale of the problem is large: as political change appeared on the horizon in 1990, foreign exchange transactions soared to more than R3-billion rands per day.

Some business leaders also favour exports because they fear AIDS will devastate local labour and consumer markets. 'As the numbers of sick and dying soar, the entire nature of the labour market will change drastically,' Nedbank's Edward Osborn has predicted. 'There is likely to be even added incentive towards mechanisation and automation... The market could shift from a volume market to a quality market. The overall ceiling to the domestic market makes it imperative to promote South African exports and to widen and strengthen the range of exports.'

As a social tragedy, AIDS will be devastating enough. But business may also use it to sink the ANC-Cosatu policy vision of labour-intensive production for local consumption.

The only hope for South African exports is to penetrate the backward, nearly bankrupt African market. But there is so little acceptable 'hard currency' north of the Limpopo that this export route appears blocked for the foreseeable future. The same appears true for the newly-opened Eastern European markets.

One solution is barter trade – also called 'countertrade'. Fred Bell, a former arms dealer for Armscor, is investigating this option for Pretoria.

Bell, who heads the Countertrade Association of South Africa, has admitted that in 1988 he was 'operating clandestinely, as the ideological walls between South Africa and the Communist bloc were still in place. But when I first visited Eastern Europe in May 1988, I found there were huge opportunities for trade by means of countertrade.'

It was perhaps uncomradely of the East Bloc to cut such deals behind the ANC's back. In any event, in mid-1990 Pretoria announced further East Bloc deals with Hungary, Rumania, Poland and Czechoslovakia.

black workers, Iscor's privatisation was a disaster, with the workforce reduced from 79 000 to 58 000. Privatisations scheduled for the early 1990s include parts of the state-owned electricity, transport and post office systems.

◆ *The export-oriented economy will increasingly divide black workers into a 30% core of skilled workers and a 70% periphery of unskilled, self-exploited, informal sector labourers.* For the 'insiders', the benefits of this division will include unprecedented mobility, relatively good wages, steady pay increases, access to housing finance, employee share ownership plans, and more opportunities for education and improving skills.

But the masses of 'outsiders' can look forward to unemployment, the informal sector, and economic survival through 'self-help'. For housing assistance, government is preparing to make available once-off site and service grants of R6 000. This will locate the outsiders in controlled peri-urban dumping grounds some geographical distance from the formal economy. Examples include Johannesburg's Orange Farm and Rietfontein.

Certainly, not all sectors of big business are aiming for these sorts of results. Indeed, strategists at the Perm, Nedbank and Old Mutual devised an alternative programme in late 1990, which appeared to have much in common with that of the ANC and Cosatu. But it remains doubtful whether South Africa's most enlightened capitalists can convince the free market econocrat ideologues to adopt an economic programme contrary to their short-term self-interest.

The imminent failure of establishment economics

Can South Africa grow using this export-oriented strategy? Can the necessary class alliances be forged, and can newly-improved social control limit disruptions by those who protest too strongly?

In spite of a strong endorsement of the strategy in an International Monetary Fund report of October 1990, these questions cannot be definitively answered in advance. But there are certainly indications that state and big business strategy will come up short in key areas.

The social contract with progressive forces is not easily forged. Urban insiders of the upper echelons of the working class, for example Numsa members, appear to be resisting big business' political project with great vigour. And land speculation – especially in areas near townships – makes it much more difficult to develop desperately-needed, affordable housing for even the top 30% of the black population.

As for the manufacturing export drive, the prospects of South African manufacturing goods competing with Far East products are not encouraging. This will be especially true in the 1990s, as a global recession fundamentally weakens markets. Even without competition and recession, exporting to international markets is getting more difficult as the three big geopolitical blocs – North America, Europe 1992, and the Japan-led Asian economic community – adopt fortress-like protectionist policies against foreign imports.

For South Africa, the international rules of 'fair play' – such as the General Agreement on Trade and Tariffs – will come increasingly into play. The International Monetary Fund will demand, and win, an end to the tariffs and other trade barriers which protect South African manufacturers from a flood of cheap imports. A huge increase in unemployment can be expected, which in turn will make the formation of a local social contract more difficult.

These hostile conditions make the future of the state–big business economic growth strategy look grim. Efforts to get ANC endorsement of the strategy may work in some areas – such as bringing in new foreign investment and applying for billions of rands in loans from the World Bank and IMF – but probably will not succeed across the board.

Economic expectations are simply too high to allow such a severe decline in formal sector employment. For the state and business ideologues, redistribution of wealth will occur through growth. The ANC and Cosatu, however, demand instead that growth occurs through redistribution.

The Great Economic Debate

The ANC claims that a post-apartheid government will not be the instrument of local or foreign big business. ANC and Cosatu economists have spelled out a programme of their own – Growth through Redistribution – and have attempted to place it high on the political agenda. They have been only partially successful.

Cosatu's Economic Trends group began developing the ideas behind Growth through Redistribution in 1987. ANC economists in London came to a similar set of broad conclusions by early 1990. A May 1990 meeting in Harare allowed the position to crystallise, although opinions differed as to particular strategies.

ANC Department of Economic Policy economists and Cosatu advisors made frequent headlines at this time. Then came numerous meetings between the ANC and business economists, mostly behind closed doors.

Following a top-level ANC–business conference in Johannesburg in May, the *Financial Mail* commented, 'The ANC is muddled and confused. It needs to be guided and educated – taught to face harsh economic reality and the need to modify the expectations of its cadres.' The *FM* called on business leaders to play a new role 'of patiently and systematically educating blacks into the economic realities of the world.' Such racist paternalism may not be characteristic of general business attitudes. ANC–business meetings apparently resulted in a common understanding which acknowledged the big business sector's powerful role in a post-apartheid South Africa.

In September 1990, another Harare meeting of ANC and Cosatu economists considered a discussion document on economic policy. The absence of previous references to nationalisation or tough anti-trust policies to dismember the conglomerates was notable.

Business Day described the document as a new 'dawn of reason' in economic thinking: 'Increasingly, the public utterances of the ANC acknowledge the need

Machines vs people

According to South African Foreign Trade Organisation officials, South Africa must engage in 'massive capital spending' to improve the quality of products for export. But new machinery must be of international quality, and that will be extremely expensive.

The solution? A special World Bank export promotion loan fund, which provides huge sums of money for manufacturers to buy state-of-the-art machines from abroad if they have a chance of exporting their products. Similar lines of credit were already being organised in mid-1990 by Swiss bankers.

Already, the meagre investments being made by South African capitalists are overwhelmingly oriented to replacing labour with machines. According to Anglo American's Clem Sunter, 'We are still moving into the knowledge-intensive 1990s where medium-sized and big businesses are shedding large pools of unskilled labour in favour of small clusters of highly skilled computer and maintenance staff who look after the robots and other automated machinery... Technology is also changing the nature of production – from mass output of identical objects to short, flexible runs of highly customised consumer goods.'

But there may be resistance to a new technology which reduces workers to robot-minders and which supports luxury, 'niche' consumption. The new computer technology fits into 'flexible' production systems of 'just-in-time' Japanese inventory control, 'quality circles' of workers and management, and subcontracting. All amount, in essence, to work *speed-up* and more intense exploitation.

Will the World Bank and IMF fail?

*P*ossibly the premier test of the ANC's economic skill and wit comes in the series of pre-liberation negotiations with the World Bank and International Monetary Fund. Here the ANC confronts the financial brain of international capitalism, the agencies responsible for lubricating the global system of trade and investment.

Through the power of debt, these Washington-based econocrats have succeeded in lowering wage rates and standards of living around the world far more efficiently than messy direct interventions by their securocrat neighbours in the CIA and Pentagon ever could.

What can South Africa expect from the commanding heights of international finance? Every ANC exile living in sub-Saharan Africa must be fully aware of how devastating IMF free market solutions can be when applied to stumbling and insecure governments. In Zambia the IMF demanded and won huge reductions in food and transport subsidies. The cuts caused riots on several occasions, and government troops killed dozens of protesters in 1986 and 1990. From the premature street celebrations, it seemed that a near coup in July 1990 was enormously popular among Zambians.

Instead of relying on such direct experience, the ANC apparently follows the sort of advice put to them by JSE President Tony Norton in October 1990: 'They must talk to people like competent economists from the IMF. If they go to Washington, they'll find that they'll be doing what Nigeria's doing, and everybody else is doing, which is privatising and reducing the state's share of the economy.'

But even in South Africa's case, talk will not be cheap, Norton concedes: 'Today we all have to take the IMF package pledge...if we want access to other funds, from other banks, the World Bank... And that package does not allow many of the things that have been spoken of in the past. But the price of freedom is discipline.'

People like Norton do not experience IMF 'discipline' in quite the same way as others. Such discipline, Third World countries have discovered, is completely ineffectual when a country confronts declining international commodity prices. Even if the discipline could pave the way for sustainable growth, the short-term costs are lethal for both poor and working people, and for hapless governments trying to enforce the free market theories of the international econocrats.

'South Africa should not be mesmerised by calls for foreign investment, boosting exports, and balancing our books,' Ben Turok, who directs the Institute for African Alternatives, concludes.

to stimulate economic growth, to maintain markets as a pricing mechanism, and to woo investors and entrepreneurs by the only known method, which is to offer security of property and opportunity of profit. Quite possibly, the economic planners have come to perceive that the creation of wealth is a separate, and different, process from the spending of wealth, just as keeping a cow is a separate and different activity from drinking milk.'

Leading ANC thinkers had started to question aspects of anti-capitalist economic strategy well before the February 1990 unbanning. The collapse of centrally-planned economies in Eastern Europe was a factor in this reassessment. But the sense that the balance of power was heavily weighed against the ANC was also important. This meant some early accommodation would be necessary with big business.

A statement by Nelson Mandela from prison in January 1990 set off an explosive debate on nationalisation and privatisation. Mandela started off with a hard-line position: in accordance with the demands of the Freedom Charter the mines, banks and monopoly corporations would be nationalised. A change in position would be 'inconceivable'.

This was fairly predictable. Many saw the nationalisation announcement as a bargaining chip, to be thrown away as political negotiations became more serious. But the pace of the backtracking was quickened by the uncompromising stance of big business.

A number of events served to warn the ANC that the corporations would not tolerate suggestions of a substantially state-run economy. There was a significant flight of capital from South Africa in February, followed by the dramatic transfer of the De Beers foreign operations headquarters to Switzerland. Mandela's June visit to the US was an important opportunity to water down the ANC nationalisation position. His reward was an extremely favourable reception from leading political and business opinion-makers.

In South Africa, big business began breathing easier about its long-term future. 'The debate around the future economy of South Africa has progressed well,' Democratic Party stalwart Denis Worrall told *Business Day* readers in an October column. 'The problem areas have been identified, the main approaches highlighted, and there is a shared determination to find answers. In fact, discussion of the nationalisation/privatisation, growth/redistribution issues has been at a world-class level.'

But The Great Economic Debate had skimmed over three crucial issues: inward versus outward growth; labour-intensive versus capital-intensive production; and the huge speculative bubble in the financial system.

Discussions on economic policy were only beginning in some quarters by October 1990: trade unions were surprised to learn that nationalisation was now essentially off the bargaining table; ANC branches had thus far found the level of debate on the mixed economy too abstract; and intellectuals from both right and left were demanding a bit more meat to the Growth through Redistribution argument. The debate on first principles was not yet over.

The left in the debate

The ANC's backtracking from a militant economic programme had much to do with building alliances during a crucial stage of the democratisation process.

But what of the longer-term debate and struggle over the sort of economy – regulated capitalism or semi-planned democratic socialism – which will best serve South Africa? What forces stand in the way of a good relationship between big business – both local and international – and the ANC?

Unions are being asked to accept certain concessions, even as the econocrats convince the ANC to maintain the economic status quo. The most difficult aspect of ANC economic policy is likely to be the rarely-mentioned, vaguely-understood notion of 'wage restraint'. Even progressive economists like Stephen Gelb have argued that it will be a necessary evil of post-apartheid economic reconstruction.

The tensions surrounding this question were thrown up during a seven-week strike at Mercedes Benz's East London factory in mid-1990. Local trade union leaders went against union policy of centralised wage bargaining, believing they would win a better package by cutting a plant-level deal. Their unwillingness to accept wage restraints suggests that organised workers may firmly oppose such policies in the future.

Perhaps not even the South African Communist Party would offer opposition to an austere ANC national wage policy. Heribert Adam, a noted establishment thinker, has claimed the SACP is 'more pragmatic concerning negotiations and the post-apartheid economy than other forces in the alliance.'

As if to prove Adam's point, an *African Communist* article by Phineas Malinga concluded that 'the application of the classical form of nationalisation to the gold mines is a project of doubtful worth.' He failed to mention that nationalisation is formal policy for the National Union of Mineworkers.

In his article, Malinga accepted crucial econocrat premises, including the need for imported capital-intensive technology, the possibility of 'significant improvement' in South African export markets, a warm welcome to foreign investors, and a surprising endorsement of 'egalitarian, up-to-date' Japanese corporate organisation. It remains unclear how widespread this position is within the SACP.

Left opposition from the Pan Africanist Congress is unlikely to materialise. Rhetoric from the PAC's youth affiliate is powerful, especially on economic policy. Yet the elders seem more flexible. Following a July 1990 meeting with the PAC in Harare, the director of South Africa's American Chamber of Commerce, Wayne Mitchell, expressed his delight. 'We noticed a far more pragmatic approach to economic issues than we have heard emanating from the ANC.'

Two months later, the PAC issued an economic policy statement which sought 'redistribution of wealth and decision-making powers at individual company levels.' PAC leader Benny Alexander termed this 'more important than nationalisation.' Policies the PAC wanted to encourage in companies, said Alexander, included worker shares in companies; affirmative action; training and development; increased corporate social responsibility; and worker involvement in

ANC economic goals

*T*he current plight of our country's economy demands an economic policy prioritising as a matter of extreme urgency the achievement of the following broad objectives:

◆ Creating new jobs and progressively eliminating unemployment;

◆ Raising real incomes, particularly for those who are most impoverished and deprived;

◆ Increasing output and productivity, particularly but not only in those sectors producing goods and services to meet the basic needs of the majority of the people;

◆ Correcting racial and gender imbalances in the economy through Affirmative Action policies;

◆ Implementing a land reform programme capable of simultaneously addressing a major national grievance, responding to the acute land hunger and increasing food production;

◆ Developing major new housing, education, health and welfare programmes capable of addressing the pressing needs in these areas;

◆ Improving the provision of infrastructure to deprived areas;

◆ Promoting greater democratic participation in economic life and a more equitable pattern of economic ownership;

◆ Creating a more democratic industrial relations framework based on full rights of workers to organise and growing participation by unions in policy formulation;

◆ Guaranteeing high standards of administration in economic affairs and ensuring that destabilising financial imbalances (eg, unmanageable budget and balance of payment deficits) do not occur;

◆ Ensuring that growth takes place in ways which harness the environment in a constructive and responsible manner; and

◆ Promoting new forms of involvement in beneficial international economic relations and co-operating with the OAU and SADCC in creating new patterns of mutually beneficial economic interaction in the southern African region and African continent.'

From Department of Economic Policy, 'Discussion Document on Economic Policy', September 1990.

company management. There was not, apparently, a broader vision of the kind of growth strategy that would result from these mainly institutional changes.

More explicitly revolutionary socialist groups, such as the Azanian People's Organisation or the Workers Organisation for Socialist Action, seem inconsequential in all but their fiery criticisms of the mainstream progressive movement. Attacking ANC economic advisers, WOSA argued that 'Proposals made by those on the left, focusing on nationalisation, on foreign exchange controls, on minimum wages, etc, are nothing more than reforms within the capitalist system that can be whittled away by a change in the balance of class forces.'

Growth through Redistribution

The September 1990 ANC discussion document spelt out the broad themes captured by the phrase Growth through Redistribution. There are certain inconsistencies in the document, but if translated into plain language, the broad argument will appeal to most poor and working people.

The ANC is clear about what it does not want: 'The engine of growth in the economy of a democratic, non-racial and non-sexist South Africa cannot be rising demand for luxury goods by a minority of wealthy consumers. Neither can we develop as a more industrial society unless our manufacturing industries can become less dependent on imported inputs paid for by mineral exports.'

This places ANC policy at variance with the current growth strategy of government and big business. Yet the ANC also acknowledges the need to 'promote industrial exports, particularly but not only to our neighbours on the African continent.' The document pledges the ANC to develop 'strategies to reintegrate South Africa into the world economy on a competitive basis and in a manner beneficial to the overall development goals.'

That sort of reintegration will be extremely difficult, unless the price of gold soars. The discussion document does not mention hostile international economic forces nor the prospect of control of the South African economy by institutions such as the International Monetary Fund.

Yet as Stephen Gelb concluded just before the ANC document was released, 'The global economy and the pressures it will impose are the biggest obstacles facing any development strategy that will try to promote equity. Because of that I'm pessimistic about the prospects for greater equity.'

There are plenty of realistic, yet simultaneously radical, features to the Growth through Redistribution proposals for national economic policy.

The ANC wants to 'use redistribution to satisfy basic needs and create new patterns of demand.' Gelb has suggested that 'what is necessary is not redistribution of consumption, but the redistribution of *investment*.' ANC and Cosatu economists differ over how this would work: 'One view suggests that the emphasis should be placed upon expanding labour-intensive light industries in the formal sector, such as food, clothing, furniture and so on, to try and take advantage of economies of scale. A contrasting view is that investment should be actively targeted towards the expansion of infrastructural services, such as electricity and telephones, to the black townships in particular.'

But whichever route is taken, says Gelb, 'housing construction is possibly the most important single sector to be targeted for investment.'

Either of these routes to Growth through Redistribution would be more progressive – in terms of generating employment and producing goods for local consumption – than the current state–big business strategy of export production on the basis of high technology machinery.

Despite Gelb's attempt to address investment, the ANC discussion document focused largely on redistribution of consumption. 'Changing the pattern of demand', in this context, means giving poor and working people the purchasing power to buy new products. The ANC also proposed a strong social welfare platform, including a national pension plan (run by the state) and a compulsory unemployment scheme (to which both employers and the state would contribute). Neither would permit discrimination against women. Funds accumulated in the pension scheme would support progressive development projects, so long as risk to the beneficiaries remained minimal.

These were the broad features of the ANC's Growth through Redistribution programme as 1990 drew to a close. Efforts were made to promote discussion of the document within ANC branches, and debates were underway in trade unions over whether too much ideological ground – especially on nationalisation – had been surrendered. While big business celebrated the breakthrough, other analysts tried to judge how the document would affect political change.

This economic programme can be seen as the left's demands for the minimal conditions in a humane post-apartheid society. Such principles are now being fought for in a variety of grassroots settings, and the next year or two will show whether the ANC discussion document resonates with popular struggles.

As that process unfolds, ANC members will be mulling over the document's contradictions – especially the importance of industrial exports in the strategy, and whether redistribution concerns mainly investment or consumption.

Could the Growth through Redistribution strategy work? The answer has much to do with the *expectations* of ANC members and supporters. Business and many liberal whites fear that poor and working people's expectations will be out of all proportion to the resources available. In the Zimbabwean experience, civil society was so poorly organised that expectations and popular demands were not taken seriously by the government after liberation. The lack of grassroots pressure permitted economic power to remain in the hands of a few whites, international financiers, and a small but important black bureaucratic class.

Had expectations in Zimbabwe been higher after 1980, more force might have been exerted on the government to redistribute land, create new jobs through public works programmes, and control the flow of speculative finance in that economy.

Gelb has conceded that Growth through Redistribution would produce a lower growth rate than the export-oriented approach of the state and big business. This pessimism is warranted in the context of the over-accumulation crisis which will remain a feature of the South African economy in the 1990s.

Some members of Cosatu's Economic Trends group refer to Growth through Redistribution as a 'second-best' scenario: if socialism is not on the agenda, it is at least a useful task for 'ex-Marxist' economists to set out how capitalism can achieve growth and at the same time provide for more basic human needs than before.

But this pessimism is unwarranted if a different understanding of the crisis – that of over-accumulation – is built into the analysis of how to restructure the economy. Such an analysis can be empowering, not disempowering, if it rests on real struggles of activists and a sense of the chaos that the crisis has produced within the commanding heights.

A logical flaw

Any South African government of the 1990s – National Party, ANC or some combination – will have to devalue over-accumulated capital, especially in the financial system. This destruction of capital must restructure both finance and the productive economy, establishing conditions for another round of growth.

Financial restructuring is especially important. It goes to the heart of the operation of the economy, involves hundreds of billions of rands, threatens worker pensions and savings, and raises the question of South Africa's links to the international economy.

Even a few business leaders – like Nedbank's Edward Osborn – occasionally acknowledge this reality: 'We've got to go through a period of economic stress, in terms of recession, retrenchment and the like. We've had the speculative fever, the preoccupation with financial assets, and I think we're coming to the end of that period. Look, I don't think we're looking at a collapse of the economy and absolute disaster. We're going through a great period of adjustment, financial adjustment. And the great risk that we're facing – in fact that's emerging – is the consequent social distress.'

Many radical economists remain pessimistic because of the constraints imposed by the over-accumulation crisis and the necessary 'financial adjustment' which the rest of the world began experiencing in earnest in 1990, and which the Third World suffered during the 1980s.

No matter how progressive their goals and policy statements, ANC and Cosatu economists have basically accepted the constraints of the over-accumulation crisis as inevitable, and have tried to construct an alternative economic strategy *around them.*

This approach has at least one crucial flaw: it assumes that a new economic system – whether Growth through Redistribution or export-led growth – can be firmly rooted before the devaluation of finance begins in earnest. This logical flaw, passed on to economic policy-makers from regulation theory, sees economic crisis as a 'turning point' rather than a period when contradictions in the system become irreconcilable and a major shake-out results.

Growth through Redistribution offers vaguely-worded reforms for South African capitalism, with a sense that only state-directed investment might 'solve' matters, and then only if big business co-operates. Its orientation towards public works programmes echoes British economist John Maynard Keynes' advice to finance ministers during the 1930s depression. Massive state intervention in the economy, Keynes argued, could act as a stimulant to offset economic stagnation. But Keynes' advice *followed* the international collapse of over-accumulated finance from 1929 to 1933.

Although 1990 was a year of devastating economic chaos across the globe, with the Japanese stock market losing half of its value and US building societies and banks failing at a brisk pace, the process of financial devaluation is not yet fully underway in South Africa.

The South African economy still faces vastly overvalued stock market shares and real estate, not to mention untenable levels of debt and extremely high interest rates. The ANC, committed to fighting inflation and beholden to high finance, might be compelled to continue these. As a result, loose capital will still be attracted to financial markets instead of into production of goods and services. Under such conditions a Keynesian solution may fall flat.

Taxes on speculation suggested by the ANC might help to cool financial fevers. But such taxes deal with symptoms not causes, and in any case have not proven successful in doing more than slightly checking speculative impulses. The problem, again, is that the financial bubble has built up too much to bring it down in any controlled way.

Realistically, the stock market must crash at some point. Real estate will go through an extraordinary shake-up that will vary tremendously across cities and regions as Group Areas Act barriers fall. The huge levels of debt could be reduced, but through unprecedented individual bankruptcies and corporate failures, which would bring some of South Africa's already-overextended banks and building societies down as well. Alternatively, dramatic inflation and low interest rates could make the debt burden more manageable, but not without increasing tensions and bottlenecks in production.

In these respects, a reformist post-apartheid economic programme will leave many people from all walks of life severely disappointed.

At core, ANC and Cosatu post-apartheid economic policy has failed to identify how the over-accumulation crisis creates new possibilities, especially for disciplining the power of high finance. The exploration of these potentials is the subject matter of Chapter Four.

ANC policy proposals

*U*nder the ANC, a post-apartheid state would be extensively over-hauled. It would extend deeply into the economy of black South Africa, attempting to be supportive yet not domineering.

Trade unions would have a 'central role in the formulation and implementation of all economic policy.' Co-operative and community based projects would be promoted and brought into the planning process.

The private sector would be encouraged to support affirmative action. If high levels of concentration in industry were judged detrimental to 'efficient and effective use of resources', reforms would be imposed, preferably 'in co-operation with business, but if such co-operation were not forthcoming a future democratic government could not shirk its clear duty in this regard.'

While some of the policy proposals listed below are subject to study and 'consideration', the range of ideas illustrates the diversity of approaches which ANC economists believe can be used to tackle problems.

*H*ousing:
◆ release affordable urban and rural land;
◆ provide infrastructural services;
◆ serviced stands made available to community-controlled housing development projects;
◆ many more low cost public housing units;
◆ encourage financial institutions to make a portion of their funds available to finance low cost housing projects.

*M*ineral resources:
◆ encourage venture capital for new mines, possibility of state investments in mines;
◆ stabilise mineral prices through formation of cartels and a state marketing authority;
◆ root out racist labour practices and improve mineworker conditions;
◆ explore options in respect of ownership patterns.

*A*griculture and land reform:
◆ immediately return land to those removed from black freehold land

or from plots held under labour tenancy agreements;
◆ provide further support to those who benefit from land reform;
◆ reallocate credit facilities, support services and training programmes according to principles of affirmative action;
◆ positively discriminate in favour of women;
◆ abolish backward labour employment practices and encourage farmworker unions;
◆ encourage rural and community organisations.

*E*nvironment:
◆ reduce current unacceptable levels of pollution;
◆ increase electrification to reduce wood and coal burning;
◆ review nuclear power programmes;
◆ prohibit dumping of toxic waste from abroad.

*H*uman resources:
◆ education, training and skills acquisition must be developed;
◆ affirmative action must be promoted both in the public and private sectors, especially for black women;
◆ empower organised labour.

*F*inancing:
◆ rationalise and restructure the financial sector;
◆ state intervention essential to correct financial deregulation and monetarist policies;
◆ possible new state-owned financial institutions and transformation of existing institutions;
◆ tax burden shifted towards corporations;
◆ possible capital gains, wealth and higher estate taxes, particularly where speculative activities are concerned;
◆ exchange controls modified;
◆ avoid large budget deficits.

*P*lanning:
◆ co-ordinate the contribution of all sectors and interest groups;
◆ involve mass-based organisations in planning and consult widely with all significant interested parties;
◆ avoid commandist or bureaucratic planning methods;
◆ local government (with single local tax base) to provide many goods and services and management infrastructure.

4

Community control

South Africa's first democratically-elected government will face enormous barriers in its attempts to build a just economy. Conglomerates will not repatriate funds they have spirited offshore, dismantle price cartels nor cease their acquisitions of other companies. They will not increase output immediately nor invest funds in new factories. The Johannesburg Stock Exchange will not transform itself into a harmless market for raising funds. Foreign investors will demand the same conditions they require from weak governments across the Third World. The environment will be badly damaged, while women will face similar impediments to those existing at present. And racism is likely to continue in many spheres of the economy.

But undue pessimism may not be warranted. For South African capitalism is in crisis not only for those toiling in mines, factories, offices and fields, but also for those at the commanding heights.

The best illustration of this lies in the speculative, over-extended financial system, already a central focus of battle between big business and poor and working people. A strong popular defence against the devaluation of over-accumulated capital as a way out of economic crisis can set the stage for longer-term community control of South Africa's economic destiny.

The promise of civil society

A number of mass struggles for progressive control of the economy have, since the late 1980s, advanced the interests of poor and working people. These struggles are most notable in the townships, the workplace and South Africa's relations with the international economy. They suggest an outline of a national strategy of 'non-reformist reform' of society, grounded in the strongest civil society in Africa.

Civil society refers to the promise and prominence of a strong *non-governmental* democratic force representing the interests of ordinary people independently of the state.

Unions are often the strongest institutions of civil society, and with a range of other organisations are best equipped to develop a broad, progressive movement independent of any future government. There is, of course, the possibility that an 'aristocracy' within the union movement becomes co-opted – and this is a key goal of big business at present.

'Community'

A community, according to dictionary definitions, is made up of any group with something in common: an organised political, municipal or social body; people living in the same locality; those with religion, profession or some other important factor in common.

The struggles waged against apartheid brought many people and groups together in a self-conscious community with an overarching purpose. This has created a solid foundation for a more democratic economy through community control.

For example, the sense of community within the broad anti-apartheid movement led unions – even those representing workers employed by multinational corporations – to support the international call for disinvestment, although this increased hardship amongst their members.

And though there have been differences on strategy and tactics within the anti-apartheid movement, especially between union 'workerists' and community 'charterists', the head of the former General Workers' Union, Johnson Mpukumpa, expressed a sentiment which soon became widespread: 'To have a good relationship and work together with the communities will also help us to have more strength. It would be a strange thing if I say I'm opposed to community associations, whilst I'm a worker from the community.' Many top unionists – Moses Mayekiso from Numsa, Cyril Ramaphosa from NUM and Chris Dlamini from Fawu – are today also leading members of their township civic associations. Their conception of community is expanding and is now best termed 'civil society'.

73

The same may also be true for leading affiliates of the United Democratic Front, which in 1990 were showered with offers of access to billions of rands in state funds – through the Independent Development Trust – and interest and attention from the Urban Foundation as part of the attempt to construct a new social contract at both local and national levels.

But regardless of how trade unions emerge from alliances negotiated by the ANC-SACP-Cosatu grouping, and regardless of whether some civic leaders adhere to the big business–Urban Foundation vision of post-apartheid cities, a broad, progressive civil society should be able to maintain itself quite independently of any future government.

This approach was strengthened when United Democratic Front leaders committed themselves to building independent township civic associations rather than merging into local branches of the ANC.

The commitment to a strong and democratic civil society was cemented in the Transvaal with the mid-1990 formation of the Civic Associations of the Southern Transvaal (Cast). And in addition to trade unions and township and regional civics, there are numerous other institutions which will be responsible for upholding civil society in a post-apartheid South Africa – block committees, youth organisations, parent and teacher educational groups, human rights bodies, the media, and even international solidarity forces.

Leading the struggle for a strong civil society are little-known activists who could have as great a role in shaping ANC economic policy as the economists whose recent papers and debates have attracted so much attention. This will be true even if they remain independent of the post-apartheid government, which increasing numbers of them seem likely to be.

These activists are at least intuitively aware of the economic constraints described in Chapter Three. South African capitalism in crisis provides both dangers and opportunities for its opponents. Perhaps without always analysing it thoroughly, radical South Africans see plenty of evidence of crisis – and as the 1990s dawn they are attempting to take enormous steps to implement a new and different economics for a new South Africa. Activists' tough-minded engagements internationally, in the workplace, and in the townships aim to alter the balance of forces.

Community control and international finance

Beginning in the late 1970s, the small but growing community of international anti-apartheid activists took some extraordinary steps in the struggle for control of South Africa's economic destiny. To increase the costs of apartheid they organised campaigns to embarrass international banks making loans to South Africa.

This took place in a period when declining corporate profits, the high cost of imported oil, the 1975-78 recession, the Soweto uprising, and the state's desire to expand major investment projects all created a dire need for foreign loans. The last-mentioned projects alone cost R13-billion from 1972-78, of which nearly R3-billion was raised from foreign bankers.

Ad hoc groups with names such as 'Committee to Oppose Bank Loans to South Africa' and 'End Loans to South Africa' sprang up in the US and Europe, working closely with the broader anti-apartheid movement. Some of their initial government-lobbying campaigns – against guaranteeing of loans by the US Export-Import Bank, or against new International Monetary Fund credits – were surprisingly successful. A few governments – especially Norway, Sweden, Nigeria and Tanzania – took strong steps against financial ties with South Africa in the 1970s. In a courageous move, Nigeria and Tanzania took action against local Barclays Bank operations because of the bank's close South Africa links.

But moving beyond governmental restrictions and into the commanding heights of the private financial sector was not an easy task. As Simon Clarke pointed out in 1980, 'International banking is a very competitive business conducted on fine profit margins. If sanctions against lending to South Africa prevented South Africa from meeting its financial obligations the result could be disastrous for some of those banks with major involvement in South Africa, with the risk of a major bank default which could have a chain reaction through national and international banking'.

Individual banks were harassed periodically by the anti-apartheid campaigners. In many cities in the US, for example, bank connections to South Africa provided activists with excellent linkages to their own local concerns. American banks were 'redlining' (discriminating against) inner-city ghettos when granting housing bonds, but at the same time making funds available to Pretoria, and this provided the evidence for many a campaign based on the theme 'Think Globally, Act Locally.'

These banks had little other than public relations to distinguish themselves from their competitors, and being smeared with the apartheid brush hurt a great deal. The British anti-apartheid movement featured thousands of student activists transferring funds from Barclays to other banks, and this plus Barclays' desire to expand to the US – where banking sanctions were strongest, and enshrined in national legislation – eventually led the bank to sell its South African operations to Anglo American.

Seeds of these local campaigns could be found in anti-bank demonstrations launched by the radical 1960s movement, Students for a Democratic Society, and their first target was the New York City headquarters of Chase Manhattan. Chase weathered a great number of such protests over the years, including sophisticated church and pension fund investment campaigns which placed formal resolutions before shareholders calling on the bank to leave South Africa. But in July 1985, with the state of emergency and the belligerence of PW Botha sending clear signals to foreign investors, Chase pulled out a $500-million line of credit to South African banks.

The resulting uproar was the strongest proof possible that sanctions worked. Botha was forced to close the JSE for fear of a meltdown; a new devalued currency

Lessons from north of the Limpopo

*T*he development experience of the rest of Africa is often cited by business and the current state to 'prove' that nationalisation, socialism, Africanisation of state bureaucracies and industry, and programmes aimed at self-reliance are pipe dreams which inevitably fail.

Many on the left also criticise the African experience of underdevelopment, locating the problems in 'neo-colonialism'. They suggest that the classes controlling African countries are by and large elites with interests opposed to poor and working people.

The African elites gained and retained power largely through repression and connections to the international political and economic system. And if many African rulers are today on the verge of losing power, the reasons mainly relate to the conditions imposed on them by international forces, especially the International Monetary Fund and World Bank. (These institutions, it is often said, have brought down more governments than the ideas of Marx and Mao.)

'With few exceptions', says Ethiopian development expert Fantu Cheru, a professor at American University in Washington, DC, 'most African leaders do not dare challenge the status quo which has served their personal economic and political interests. The tripartite alliance between the African state, local elites and western interests continues to impede the process of democratisation at the national level.'

If African countries did threaten international economic elites, even if only ideologically, they often came under both military and economic attack.

Even exceptionally subservient African elites faced economic strangulation because of conditions in international markets they had no control over. From late 1979, for example, interest rates on international bank loans soared, and a global recession flattened demand for African goods. As a result, the value of the raw materials and other basic commodities that African countries exported declined by 40% from 1980-87. After 1984, Third World countries began repaying more in interest on old loans than they received in new loans. By 1989, the difference was an astounding $50-billion in yearly debt payments draining from South to North.

Reacting to these conditions, a group of African economists released a statement in London in 1987 which took the principle of community control to the national level. They suggested some important steps in clarifying progressive rules of engagement with the international economy:

"1. The African people must continue to expose the inequities of the present international economic, political and social order, and demand full democratic participation in those organisations which make decisions relating to the ordering of international society, and the allocation of resources.

2. The African people must demand a fair and just return for the production of their labour in the international market, and reject international pricing and marketing arrangements which undervalue the products of African labour.

3. The African people must reject development projects imposed on our people either by international agencies or by our own leaders when they serve external interests rather than the interests of the ordinary people of Africa. Sometimes, these projects are suggested by foreign private and governmental interests to solve their problems rather than those of Africa.

4. The people of Africa, especially those in the low categories of society, must democratically decide their own development priorities. In pre-colonial Africa, people always placed food as the highest priority, whilst today the priorities are externally determined and people in Africa die for lack of food. These priorities must be put right.

5. In the context of rural development, we must emphasise the parallel and interconnected development of agriculture and industry so that, while agriculture provides food and raw materials for industry, the latter provides the necessary means of production to service agriculture. The initiatives to plan this kind of strategy must rest with the people themselves, and not be imposed by any outside agency or government.

6. When it comes to food production, due regard must be paid to the fact that the bulk of the food producers in Africa are women. Therefore, their legal rights to land, as well as their right to participate fully in all decision-making and allocation of resources must be respected and recognised.

7. Development projects in African countries must first and foremost service the needs of the national and local markets. Hence, the provision of inputs, credit facilities, water for irrigation, road network and storage facilities, electric power and telecommunications and extension services must first and foremost service the demands of products produced for local markets rather than for export markets.

8. We must reject the type of industrialisation which is externally-oriented, and which only serves to provide a market for imported machinery, and jobs for foreign technical and managerial experts. Our industrial strategy must be internal and African-oriented, not only to service the direct needs of our people, but also to employ our own material and human resources.

9. People must be represented directly in all democratic institutions from the village level to the national level. Without a thoroughgoing democratic method of work, decisions will always be made in the name of the people rather than by them. Hence, we must demand consistent and thorough democratisation of all institutions of decision-making.

10. The African people can enjoy full democratic rights of participation only if their human rights and liberties are recognized. People must have full freedom to express themselves politically, to form associations and trade unions, to participate in all political activities without fear of repression, and to choose their own leaders. Only by a full and thoroughgoing practice of democracy and people participation at all forums can there be any hope of getting Africa out of its present crisis. All other efforts so far tried at international or local levels are mere palliatives and attempts to tackle the symptoms of the crisis, rather than its causes."

– the financial rand – was re-introduced to stem the torrent of capital flight; and a debt repayment 'standstill' was declared. US bankers fled South Africa in droves, and although some European banks held on temporarily, the end of South Africa's access to new international loans was certain.

Those at the commanding heights often acknowledge that this was the single most important event in bringing South African bureaucrats and businesspeople to the realisation that they would have to share some degree of power with the black majority.

But the pressure was not over. The ANC monitored the subsequent rollover of South Africa's foreign debt in early 1986 and mid-1987, and by late 1988 had devised an international programme to prevent banks from bailing out Pretoria in June 1990, when the repayment pressure would be strongest.

Anti-apartheid bank campaigns were launched in international financial centres, at the ANC's behest, throughout 1989. By the time of the IMF-World Bank meetings in October 1989, a US banker told *Business Day* that 'To be seen dealing with South Africa is equivalent to being tested positive for AIDS.'

Reserve Bank Governor Chris Stals and Finance Minister Barend du Plessis managed to escape the debt trap shortly afterwards. International banks were so concerned to avoid the heat of sanctions pressure that they agreed to a rescheduling of the debt nine months early. South Africa was thus bailed out; the financial sanctions campaign had stumbled; and De Klerk entered the 1990s in a stronger position than he otherwise would have done.

Yet the lessons, even from defeat, are clear. The international community of anti-apartheid activists had mobilised behind the ANC programme of international financial isolation of South Africa. They recognised the power that international finance had over South Africa, and attempted to intervene to force progressive change on Pretoria through the weapon of popular protest.

This intervention showed how the commanding heights of the economy could be disciplined, and how community control of capital could extend to the loftiest peaks of international finance.

The most important lesson of the October 1989 bailout may well be the refusal of the international banks to support the ANC in its time of need. It could be argued that this refusal provides a rationale for classifying $20-billion of South Africa's foreign debt as 'apartheid debt'. There are cases where the inheritance of 'unjust debt' has been questioned in international courts, and the ANC may well feel it has a moral case for refusing to repay. But would this tactic help or hurt the ANC's programme for a more progressive economy?

Post-apartheid control of international finance

The international anti-apartheid community's struggle to control high finance teaches an important lesson: international financiers have both extraordinary power and a certain vulnerability. That power includes the control of entire national economies. Yet the vulnerability of international banks is clear as the 1990s unfold.

If the first post-apartheid government took a firm line on the international debt crisis, that could spur other debtors into action. Financial reporter Alec Hogg interviewed South African bankers who in 1986 believed that 'a South African default will give the excuse which countries like Argentina, Brazil and a host of other debtors need to refuse repayment themselves.'

That, according to Hogg, 'would probably cause the collapse of the Western world's financial system, pushing the gold price – and with it South Africa's economic prospects – into orbit.'

Defaulting on the apartheid debt could benefit both South Africa and countries north of the Limpopo, struggling for a chance of sustainable development.

'The most appropriate and effective strategy that Africa can undertake', insists Fantu Cheru, 'exists in its own ecology and culture. Authentic development in Africa must, therefore, emphasise cultural identity, self-reliance, social justice and ecological balance. One important precondition for fundamental change in Africa is the need to end the negative transfer of resources from the continent to the West. This can only be achieved through collective default.'

South Africa is more industrialised than other countries on the continent, and has a brighter economic future. Yet Cheru's analysis of sustainable development applies equally well here. And increasingly important social movements in Brazil, Mexico, the Philippines and elsewhere may be positioned to force their governments to support a Third World debtors' cartel.

Those at the commanding heights of international finance would certainly oppose this move and quickly end new loans, short-term trade credits and possibly even trade itself. But if the ANC becomes serious about a self-reliant economy and meeting basic needs, such sanctions should not seriously curb progressive development.

There are intense pressures on the ANC not to follow this course. But the pressure exerted from below to use resources for development rather than repayments to western bankers may one day be greater.

Community control and corporate power

South Africa's debt crisis involved more than government-guaranteed foreign loans. Corporations and consumers had started borrowing at a record pace in 1979, and high corporate debt was one indication that the South African economy was in crisis.

Simultaneously, corporations became more centralised, more international, and more sophisticated in their dealings with unions and their members.

Labour required a sophisticated response, and the combination of intensified shopfloor action and labour-community solidarity appeared to provide that. A special focus on 'campaigns' was adopted, and with it the beginnings of an action-oriented approach to control of the economy.

Mass action was the key to the success of the campaigns, whether against state repression and legislation, or corporate power. Community support for union

Campaigning against Barlow Rand

Barlow Rand is a good example of concentrated economic power. Barlow chief Mike Rosholt has engaged in extensive public relations efforts and currently he is the chair of the Urban Foundation. However, his company is known in union circles as a leader in repressive corporate behaviour – including cancelled recognition agreements and bugging of union offices. The Barlow subsidiary Nampak was known to be behind the 1989 move to destroy the printing industrial council, the body responsible for central bargaining.

Cosatu 'declared war' on Barlow Rand in January 1990 when it appeared the conglomerate would maintain its stance against centralised bargaining.

Paperworkers at Nampak went on strike later in the year, kicking off a series of solidarity actions. These included direct boycotts of Nampak products in South Africa and Europe, campaigns against companies which purchase from Nampak, efforts to block transport and handling of Nampak goods, work stoppages across Barlow Rand, and marches and pickets. These tactics aim to hit a conglomerate wherever it is weakest.

Barlow Rand is also R3,5-billion in debt. This means the company is under pressure to repay its lenders instead of acceding to worker demands. But the situation also makes Barlows vulnerable to worker-community campaigns against the company's bankers.

struggles such as the mid-1990 OK Bazaars strike was crucial at a time when pressure on trade union rights left many union staff with lower confidence in worker power than before. The difference between 1990 and conditions earlier in the decade – when some unions advised members to avoid community struggles – could not have been greater.

For example, Cosatu's struggle against privatisation has involved a broadly-based campaign against corporate power. Under privatisation, according to a Cosatu organiser, 'The aims of the enterprises are changed from providing a service to providing profit... (T)he prices of services will increase and those who can't afford to pay for services will not receive them.' Thus, all poor and working people have a material interest in joining with the workers directly affected by the privatisation of companies.

The ANC and a variety of other forces have supported Cosatu's anti-privatisation struggle. For example, when FW de Klerk suggested that the R2-billion Independent Development Trust could be partly funded through the proceeds of privatisation, community leaders successfully demanded that the privatisation link be severed.

As a result of this effort from a broad coalition, Pretoria backtracked quite noticeably from privatisation during 1990, and plans for Eskom's sale were reportedly shelved.

A proposed workers' charter traces a clear path for control of capital, according to the Cosatu organiser cited above: 'The right to join trade unions, to a living wage, to education, training and skills upgrading are demands that all workers would agree with. They are issues that workers have been struggling for over the years. They are our demands to the bosses and the state.'

Striking workers would be protected from scabs, dismissals and interdicts, and have rights to picket, call boycotts and hold sympathy strikes. To support new union organising, Cosatu wants to protect, at the very minimum,

◆ the right of shop stewards to carry out their duties;
◆ the right of access to factories for trade union organisers;
◆ the right to stop order facilities; and
◆ the right to information about companies.

If those demands are enshrined as rights in a new constitution and upheld in practice, they will make a crucial difference to the functioning of the post-apartheid economy.

There are other real opportunities for long-term bids by organised workers and non-union township residents to join forces around issues affecting them. One area where the power of workers and the development needs of communities are beginning to merge is in the use of pension and provident funds. According to the Cosatu organiser, the union federation is 'unhappy about the fact that workers contribute their money to the fund and it is then invested in banks and big companies. It is not used to serve the needs of workers. Cosatu believes that the money should be used to build homes, create employment or provide training.' Whether worker funds will take a leading role in progressive development efforts

Campaigns for control of multinational capital

When multinational corporations began withdrawing from South Africa in the mid-1980s, they did so in a way that hurt workers and helped local management. Control of multinational corporate behaviour became a crucial concern of, among others, the Chemical Workers Industrial Union, which led discussions within Cosatu on the issue, and launched a campaign that won an enormous victory against Mobil oil company in 1989.

'From the start,' explained a union organiser, 'a major concern of the campaign was to ensure that the social wealth of the people of South Africa should remain in the country. A major demand was that the proceeds of any disinvestment should be placed into a trust fund nominated by the union for social investment.'

The struggle against Mobil lasted three months and involved strikes, British and US solidarity actions, court battles and negotiations.

The union won disclosure of company information never made public before, pledges that workers would have employment security after disinvestment, and maintenance of union status with Gencor, new owners of Mobil in South Africa.

Unions have recently proposed that a future government should impose a code of conduct on multinationals, with strict provisions relating to health and safety, the environment, labour-management relations, profit repatriation and control of technology.

remains to be seen. But there is general agreement that such investments are a crucial component of community-controlled development.

Aside from control of the corporation, is greatly increased worker control at the point of production possible? Some enlightened business leaders such as Anglo American's Clem Sunter's claim that new technologies and ideas like 'quality circles' (consultations between labour and management) will make South African industry more democratic, and shopfloor relations more co-operative.

With the assistance of Economic Trends group economists, Cosatu leaders are having discussions about how best to respond to the state and big business programme of economic restructuring. Their objective is to figure out how to use the changing techniques of capitalism to advance worker control at the point of production.

But critics worry that this is playing capital's game, for the reason that the restructuring of most of South African industry is ultimately not going to help local poor and working people as consumers, but is instead geared to making South Africa internationally competitive in manufacturing goods.

It is true, of course, that establishment thinkers from Democratic Party chief Zach de Beer to planning Minister Hernus Kriel have publicly conceded that white South Africans are too rich in relation to what the country can afford. This is merely stating the obvious, but what does it mean in practice? The National Party is telling white local authorities to prepare to share tax revenues with townships, for example, and this is commendable. But the broader NP economic strategy will have the opposite effect, helping insiders and hurting already-disadvantaged outsiders.

What the majority of black South Africans call for is an economic programme aimed at *basic needs*: the houses, services (electricity, water, sewage), simple home appliances, clothing and food that are minimal requirements for leading a decent life, and that more than half the population are denied under the present system.

The good news is that essentially all of the materials and machinery needed to produce these basic commodities are available within South Africa. Thus, 'self-reliance' is no pipe-dream.

At the same time, more sophisticated products consumed by upper-class whites (and some blacks) must be reassessed, on grounds that they require too much foreign currency and are superfluous luxuries during a time of reparation. And does South Africa really need to compete with East Asian exporters in other high-tech manufacturing industries, when so much remains to be done at home?

It should be clear that with more sensitivity to basic needs, the full-fledged restructuring of many sectors of industry, along the lines suggested by the likes of Clem Sunter, becomes less urgent. Restructuring should instead occur in a way that would emphasise production of the basic developmental goods that communities are demanding.

To the degree that Cosatu can force changes in what is produced, rather than leaving this question to the market, it will have succeeded in its mission of restructuring South African industry in a progressive direction. Worker control of the means of production, in this sense, is perfectly compatible with the broader vision of community control of the local economy.

Community control and township development

Struggles for community control of capital are underway in a number of cities and towns across the country. The politics of anti-apartheid protest began to shift perceptibly in 1990, as negotiations took centre stage at both national and local levels. The politics of development appeared on the horizon, and it became important for civic leaders to understand the new developmental forces operating on their communities.

Throughout the 1980s, the state tried to pull away from direct provision of black housing, giving private developers the incentives to make townships housing profitable.

This strategy was launched in the late 1970s with the introduction of leasehold housing. It was advanced by the deregulation of building societies and the extension of various kinds of housing subsidy schemes to blacks in the 1980s.

Major building and financial companies entered the market after township protests were repressed during 1985-86, attracting the top 10% of the market. The Urban Foundation's Loan Guarantee Fund, a Perm housing bond tied to the borrower's income, and the use of pension funds as collateral for housing finance – all initiated in late 1990 when it appeared the new homes market in the township had become saturated – appeared to open the door for private housing to reach another 30-40% of the black population.

Township resistance to the state and big business changed as these conditions evolved. In the first place, organisers found the consumer boycott to be a good weapon against local government. It was used with devastating effect in Boksburg, Carletonville and Port Alfred to force local companies to change their white councils' township policies. In 1990 the South African Chamber of Business responded by suggesting counter-strategies to more than 100 chambers of commerce and industry, representing 35 000 companies.

Civic associations initially responded to the private sector's new-found interest in township development with deep mistrust. The Urban Foundation had been considered to be an enemy of progressive forces, notwithstanding its extensive house-building efforts which accounted for a quarter of all formal black housing during the late 1980s. But when trade unions began listing housing as one of their bottom-line demands of big business in the late 1980s, the question shifted from *whether* the private sector should be permitted to operate in townships to *under what conditions* this should take place.

This symbolised the shift from protest politics to the politics of community-controlled development. But it also reflected the problems the private sector was causing township residents in the late 1980s. Privatised housing involved higher monthly bond repayment rates for many residents, who then passed on the added costs to their backyard tenants. In some areas, the increases were 300% and more.

Community control of capital in Alexandra

*T*he Alexandra Civic Organisation (ACO) was relaunched in 1989 after a long treason trial of its leaders ended in their acquittal. During February 1990 the civic mobilised almost 80 000 Alexandrans in a march for better housing.

ACO campaigns under the banner of 'Affordable Housing for All in Alexandra', and has attempted to integrate the poor into general concerns about the quality of life in Alexandra.

As ACO explained in a pamphlet, 'In Alexandra, many people are living in shacks in overcrowded yards and in "squatter" areas. There are not enough proper services such as water, toilets and electricity for all in Alexandra. In the hostels, the rooms are very overcrowded, and the conditions are very poor. There are also too few schools, creches, sports fields and shops.'

When an area near Alexandra known as 'the Far East Bank' was offered to developers in July 1990, ACO proposed to the Transvaal Provincial Administration that the land be turned into a Community Land and Housing Trust through which all Alexandrans could control the destiny of their new community.

ACO has argued that community development needs to occur with certain key principles in mind: 'Residents should have direct control of the land on the Far East Bank themselves. This is to stop the land from becoming too expensive, and to stop private developers from building expensive houses that people cannot afford.

'Residents should participate in making decisions about what sorts of houses should be built on the Far East Bank. The Community Trust would own the Far East Bank, and make sure that only houses that are affordable for the people of Alexandra are built on the land. The Community Trust would supervise the building of houses and other facilities on the Far East Bank, and would try to raise the necessary finances for such a project.

'Democratic structures need to exist throughout Alexandra. We need to make sure that the yard and street committees are built, and that people join the ACO and other progressive organisations. The ACO does not just want to build houses on the Far East Bank, but build a united community as well.'

Other community development principles ACO intends applying to the Far East Bank land include skills training, job creation, building co-operatives, community control of financing, and new forms of local government.

This led to tensions and conflicts within township organisations. In Alexandra, for example, a separate community structure was formed representing more conservative middle-class homeowners.

Shoddy construction of new housing was also a problem. Even reputable developers regularly skimped on materials and failed to follow rudimentary building guidelines. This was especially true once the top 10% of township populations – who could afford houses worth more than R35 000 – had been saturated.

Below R35 000, standards for township housing were of necessity lower. But in most new housing developments standards fell far too low. When residents moved in, they discovered that finishing touches were missing, and within months found huge cracks in walls. They had little recourse, and developers often took the money and ran, never to be tracked down again.

Tensions in the economy trickled down and left black housing consumers financially over-extended. Inflation in building materials was rampant, with leading architects and developers angrily objecting to the materials cartel. The high price of land – a result of speculation – also increased private housing costs. The general tendency in the economy is to value land more than production of goods, and investors have been buying land near townships cheaply and trying to earn a large profit on resale.

But the major reason private township development has become prohibitively expensive is the enormous increase in interest rates. From 12,5% in early 1988 to 21% in late 1989, the rise of the housing bond rate has done more to bankrupt township homebuyers than any other factor.

The response of the most sophisticated sectors of the community is instructive. Bond boycotts were their first and most powerful line of defence. In townships in the Eastern and Western Cape, communities searched out the nearest target: the building societies and banks to which they paid a large monthly repayment.

In some cases that repayment had soared to unmanageable levels, and bond boycotts became both a political and practical response to economic crisis.

By mid-1990 residents in Khayalitsha and Old Crossroads had won a victory. Financiers agreed to reschedule home loans, cut monthly payments down, and pressure developers to ensure that houses were better-built.

New homeowners realised that they had some power over the country's most sophisticated financial institutions. This was the essence of community control of capital: threatening the institutions with bond boycotts and then resolving the boycott on terms more favourable than those previously existing.

Community control of local state and economy

Late in 1990, the Civic Associations of the Southern Transvaal issued a set of demands indicating the high priority it placed on community control:
◆ Racial local government structures should be disbanded and replaced with a system of single tax bases in townships and cities;

◆ One-person, one-vote municipal elections should be called for non-racial municipalities;

◆ All service-charge arrears run up during the rent boycott should be written off and houses transferred to those who had already paid for the houses through years of rent;

◆ Community trust funds should be established to pay for new housing construction;

◆ All development schemes by the private and public sectors should have community participation; and

◆ Hostels should be converted into family units and shacks developed into formal housing.

Cast and its allies in civic associations across South Africa began a militant protest campaign in support of these demands, rather than waiting for national political leaders to act on them. This sort of action offers the best prospect for community control of local government and economy to be maintained beyond political liberation. Failure to maintain pressure could result in the sort of outcomes found in Zimbabwe, where the commanding heights were not fundamentally altered once a new government was in place.

Control of the commanding heights?

Whatever the international policies pursued by the ANC in power, whatever successes unions achieve in particular campaigns, and whatever strides are made by township residents in organising democratic development, the concept of community control cannot stop there. By winning victories, raising public awareness, building self-confidence, and developing a better understanding of the forces operating from the level of the commanding heights, leaders of the communities described in this chapter are positioning themselves to play a crucial role in the post-apartheid economy.

Could these principles be applied to running the national economy, including the planning of production and distribution of goods and some sort of free-floating price system under principles of community-controlled development?

At this point, community control of hundreds of billions of rands of output is hard to envisage, but there are steps which could bring this ideal closer to reality:

◆ *Anti-trust regulations could be strengthened* so that it is illegal not only to abuse monopoly power but even to possess it. Some ANC economists have argued that it is easier to control the actions of a hundred medium-sized firms than six enormous ones. Vella Pillay, who spent many years as an executive of the Bank of China, has called for 'legislation to curb monopoly power and where necessary dismember some of the key conglomerates, to bring industrial development closer to the dictates of social need and the market.' Existing legislation and the Competition Board pose little threat to monopoly corporations, and major changes will be required if they are to be controlled or broken up.

◆ Pillay has also put forward a strong argument for 'the *involvement of the state,*

Zimbabwe – the commanding heights intact

With a strong anti-imperialist bent and an official Marxist-Leninist ideology, Zimbabwe's ruling party was expected to pose a serious challenge to local and international financiers. But the IMF and World Bank were able to dictate economic policy on matters ranging from import controls to price subsidies and government spending. Any potential for community control of capital was blocked by the country's big banks.

Zimbabwe's banks remain racially-biased institutions, ineffectual in supporting real development.

Throughout the 1980s the banks prospered, and employment in the financial sector increased by 35%; finance trailed only health and education as the fastest-growing sector in the economy. But the banks had difficulty finding borrowers who would use their funds for productive investments in plant and equipment, and loans shifted more and more into speculation or other non-productive investments. The stock market and real estate in Harare are even more speculative than in Johannesburg.

Between 1980 and 1983 bank loans to other financial institutions doubled to Z$70-million. Then in mid-1984, banks led a massive Harare property speculation boom and real estate price hike by injecting an unprecedented Z$70-million into mortgage bonds over six months.

By 1989, the Zimbabwean government reported that only 3% of bank loans were going to black borrowers in a country that is 99% black. Despite their unusually high profits, the local banks failed to grant loans to blacks where they were most needed, and where government policy is most dependent upon private sector support: rural areas, growth points and emergent businesses.

Adam Kara, who heads the Bozimo Trade and Development Corporation, called attention to 'continuous sentiments vociferously aired by the majority of our citizens, that private banks and financial institutions are not responsive to their economic goals and aspirations. A level of intolerance is being reached for their arrogance, pomp and ceremony, splendour and grandeur in the urban areas, and their indifference and obliviousness to the plight of our rural folk.'

The bottom line, though, is that the Zimbabwe government, taking orders from the World Bank, has begun *deregulating* the banks. This may well mean increasing irresponsibility among those who control Zimbabwe's economy.

the workforce, local authorities and where possible, direct consumers on the boards of directors of corporations. The state would be critical in exercising influence on the flow of investment, the distribution of income and generally the direction of the economy.'

Others have suggested the use of state power to reward corporations which are 'socially responsible', especially in supporting affirmative action and the programmes of trade unions and communities. It is doubtful whether board membership, regulations and incentives can alter the behaviour of huge companies operating according to the logic of profit, but even the task of limiting the actions of the biggest firms can educate and prepare workers for more radical transformation of the commanding heights in coming rounds of struggle.

◆ *Tax policy* could be used in creative ways to control the commanding heights. In addition to the tasks of ending race and gender discrimination in taxation and benefits, measures could be taken to ensure that big companies cease avoiding taxes, which many observers see as a serious problem at present.

According to ANC advisor Laurence Harris, a professor of economics at the University of London, 'The greatest difficulty facing the Ministry of Finance will be ensuring that the great multinationals operating in South Africa do not transfer their profits abroad by false invoicing and other types of false transfer pricing. Transfer pricing is used by multinationals all over the world to evade taxation in countries where it is relatively high, or to evade foreign exchange controls and other restrictions.'

◆ According to Harris, *post-apartheid planning* could be managed efficiently and without grotesque bureaucracies developing. Certain areas – like the prices and markets for food, foreign exchange and credit – are ripe for more active planning than even the fairly direct interventions Pretoria has made for decades. Limited but hard-hitting planning in these areas, according to Harris, is crucial since 'it leaves room for price adjustments to help prevent the worst market imbalances, and it reduces the burden a comprehensive planning system places on administrative resources.' Food pricing plans seem especially important in a country which has enormous numbers of people on the verge of starvation.

◆ *The financial system could be controlled* through a number of mechanisms: financiers could have 'prescribed asset' requirements so that a portion of their investments promote development; low-interest funding could be funnelled through government to support development finance; the Reserve Bank could be ordered to maintain interest rates low enough to help borrowers at the expense of creditors; and measures could be taken to halt speculation.

There are problems with relying on these sorts of controls to gain some leverage at the commanding heights: they represent a shifting of deck chairs on the financial Titanic since they do not address the deep roots of the crisis in over-accumulation; and the only opportunity to implement them will be after a dramatic shift in political power.

This does not mean that progressive activists and intellectuals should cease debating the pros and cons of managing and controlling the commanding heights.

But it does suggest that posing reforms of the current system should be accompanied by more radical analysis and practice.

This means greater efforts to locate and to take advantage of the economic system's most immediate vulnerabilities, which, it appears, lie primarily in the realm of high finance. From a historical point of view, this is not surprising. Through the recent financial sanctions drive, corporate campaigns and bond boycotts, activists have recognised the value of this subtle but crucial approach to capitalist crisis. After all, the problems at the commanding heights are too great to allow even the most sophisticated conglomerates an easy escape.

One indication is Anglo American's failed attempt to take over Consolidated Gold Fields in 1989 – Consgold's managing director described the takeover bid as 'financial terrorism' – which revealed that not even the strongest international connections can help a cash-rich company from a pariah country resolve its own over-accumulation crisis.

The lifting of sanctions and growing international respectability may open a few doors previously shut to Anglo, De Beers, Rembrandt, etc, but the deeper crisis of speculation, international recession, increasing global competition and protectionism, and popular resistance will remain.

These contradictions mean that even the largest firms will be too weak, economically, to provide the jobs and goods needed by the majority of poor and working people. This will be even more true when devaluation of over-accumulated capital begins in earnest in the early to mid-1990s. If the crisis continues, conglomerates could well become politically weaker too, creating a vacuum at the commanding heights of the economy. It may be that this vacuum can only be filled by widespread public ownership.

Nationalisation

Certain industries – construction materials, for example – probably require an immediate radical shake-up to allow something as important as a mass housing programme to proceed, and nationalisation may be one way of effecting this. Financial institutions, especially insurance companies, are also possible short-term targets, in view of their mutual ownership form which could allow a new government simply to replace current small boards of directors with men and women whose values more accurately reflect the interests of the masses.

Laurence Harris goes further: 'The economic case for nationalising Anglo American would rest to a large extent on the view that the huge power it has shown itself to have to shape economic development through its disposition of the surplus, should be under the control of the state. And a similar case can be made for nationalising the banks and other giant conglomerates.'

Further arguments for nationalisation rest on the social aspects of corporate South Africa, especially in the mines. 'Employment practices – hiring, firing, the organisation of production, and provision of training and housing – are based upon racial divisions and are at the heart of apartheid,' Harris comments. 'Nationalisation can be justified on the grounds that radical changes in the way these enterprises operate are necessary in order to eradicate apartheid at its roots.' This is also the basis for the National Union of Mineworkers demand for nationalisation of the mines.

Harris rejects the argument that nationalisation inevitably leads to inefficiency. 'The theoretical basis for such a view is weak. It rests on the argument that only the profit motive can stimulate management and employees of large corporations to produce at minimum cost. But modern theories of the private firm suggest it may not operate in a profit-maximising way, while the operating rules of nationalised industries can induce cost minimisation.'

The problem of compensating previous owners is raised frequently, but Harris insists that the democratic state could manage this by issuing long-term bonds in the manner the British Labour Party did in the post-war era. More radical advocates of nationalisation have argued that capitalists have made enough money already, and do not deserve compensation.

Conclusion

It is high time to construct a radical but well-reasoned approach to the post-apartheid economy, grounded in real struggles for community control of capital. This book is only a small step along that road. In the first chapter the legacy of apartheid was spelled out. In the second, the economic crisis was explained. In the third, various future directions of the economy were explored. And in this chapter the possibilities and actual practices of resisting the current powers in control of the economy were outlined.

Whether a future government – ANC led or not – follows the more radical ideas for controlling the commanding heights is a question of power. The economic power so firmly concentrated at the commanding heights might overwhelm any state and community effort to gain control.

This has been the case throughout South Africa's economic history. Continually shaping that history were the ancestors of the banks and mining houses which retain so much clout today. Certainly in the twentieth century, the economic, and not merely political, power of government also came into play. But the result of allowing *capitalist economic logic* – highly biased by racism – to determine the vast part of production, distribution, exchange and consumption, was always the same: economic crisis.

That crisis often produced a backlash, and, appropriately enough, the financial institutions that guide money and credit flows were often the principal targets of popular rage. It is clear the 1990s are no different, since direct command over much of the economy rests with financial institutions, which are themselves generally controlled by or working closely with mining conglomerates.

This offers South African progressives a crucial opportunity. In the context of massive financial devaluation it may be possible to move quickly and convincingly away from speculation and parasitic behaviour. Any danger to the long-term viability of the manufacturing, mining and agricultural sectors of the South African economy can be minimised with an offensive against high finance, where the most powerful and yet simultaneously vulnerable peaks of the commanding heights can be scaled with increasing vigour.

Here the lessons from other struggles – international financial sanctions, corporate campaigns and bond boycotts – are invaluable. Turning these diverse efforts at community control of capital into a full-fledged restructuring of the commanding heights will remain the most important challenge to follow formal democratisation.

Ultimately, after centuries of racial, gender and class oppression, the only satisfying South African democracy will be one where non-racial, non-sexist *economic democracy* can be established beyond any shadow of a doubt.